WALCH PUBLISHING

D0521188

Daily Warm-Ups

U.S. HISTORY

Kathy Sammis

Level I

The classroom teacher may reproduce materials in this book for classroom use only.
The reproduction of any part for an entire school or school system is strictly prohibited.
No part of this publication may be transmitted, stored, or recorded in any form
without written permission from the publisher.

1   2   3   4   5   6   7   8   9   10
ISBN 0-8251-6077-4
Copyright © 2006
J. Weston Walch, Publisher
P.O. Box 658 • Portland, Maine 04104-0658
www.walch.com
Printed in the United States of America

Table of Contents

Introduction . . . . *iv*

The Americas and Colonization 1

The American Revolution and the New Nation 42

Expansion and Reform 72

Civil War and Reconstruction 89

Changes in the U.S.: 1870 to the 1900s 113

Modern America Emerges: 1890 to 1930 128

The Great Depression and WWII 151

Postwar and Contemporary U.S. 160

Answer Key 181

The *Daily Warm-Ups series* is a wonderful way to turn extra classroom minutes into valuable learning time. The 180 quick activities—one for each day of the school year—practice social studies skills. These daily activities may be used at the very beginning of class to get students into learning mode, near the end of class to make good educational use of that transitional time, in the middle of class to shift gears between lessons—or whenever else you have minutes that now go unused.

Daily Warm-Ups are easy-to-use reproducibles—simply photocopy the day's activity and distribute it. Or make a transparency of the activity and project it on the board. You may want to use the activities for extra-credit points or as a check on the social studies skills that are built and acquired over time.

However you choose to use them, *Daily Warm-Ups* are a convenient and useful supplement to your regular lesson plans. Make every minute of your class time count!

Daily Warm-Ups: U.S. History

North America's Environment

North America can be divided into different environmental regions. Next to each region listed below, write a few words that sum up its basic climate.

1. Arctic _____

2. Northwest Coast _____

3. Southwest _____

4. Great Plains _____

5. Southeast _____

6. Great Forest _____

1

© 2006 Walch Publishing

American Origins

Below are some statements about the earliest people and animals of the Americas. Decide if each one is true (**T**) or false (**F**). Write the correct letter on the line. Rewrite any false statements to make them true.

_____ 1. Most of the earliest Americans crossed over to North America via a land bridge called Beringia.

_____ 2. Some of the earliest Americans may have come over from Asia in boats, crossing the Pacific Ocean.

_____ 3. Native Americans did not learn to domesticate animals until the Europeans arrived with their domesticated animals.

_____ 4. Masses of ice covered North and Central America 10,000 years ago.

_____ 5. The earliest Americans existed almost entirely on plant foods.

_____ 6. Animals in the Americas in the earliest years of human habitation were enormously larger than in more modern times.

2

© 2006 Walch Publishing

Daily Warm-Ups: U.S. History

North American Landforms

Landforms are the physical features of Earth's surface. North America has many striking landforms. Several types of landforms are listed below. For each one, name at least two major examples in North America.

Mountains

_____

_____

Rivers

_____

_____

Lakes

_____

_____

Bays/Gulfs

_____

_____

Plains

_____

_____

3

© 2006 Walch Publishing

American Places

The early civilizations in the Americas were centered in a variety of locations. Choose the correct place-name from the box to complete each sentence below.

Cahokia	Tenochtitlán	Mesa Verde
Great Lakes	Cuzco	Tikal

1. The Anasazi built and lived in a 200-room pueblo at
   _____.

2. Up to 10,000 people lived at _____, the center of the last Mound Builder culture.

3. The Maya built the great city of _____ in what is Guatemala today.

4. Five tribes of the eastern _____ region formed the Iroquois League.

5. About 200,000 people lived in the Aztec capital city of _____, built on an island in Lake Texcoco.

6. _____ was the grand and stately capital of the Inca Empire.

© 2006 Walch Publishing

Maya, Aztec, and Inca

The Maya, Aztec, and Inca each had a distinct culture. Yet these three cultures shared some elements. Label each cultural element listed below with an **M** if it applies to the Maya, an **A** if it applies to the Aztec, and/or an **I** if it applies to the Inca.

_____ 1. had a writing system

_____ 2. built huge temples

_____ 3. used rich gold resources to make ornamental objects

_____ 4. engaged in ritual ball play

_____ 5. practiced ritual human sacrifice

_____ 6. built large cities

_____ 7. society was divided into strict social classes

_____ 8. handicrafts featured the jaguar motif

_____ 9. revered a feathered serpent god

_____ 10. developed an accurate calendar

5

© 2006 Walch Publishing

Mesoamerican Events

The following statements about events in Mesoamerica are out of order. Number them from 1 to 8 in the order in which they happened, with 1 being the earliest event.

_____ The Aztecs move south into the Valley of Mexico.

_____ The Zapotec dominate the Oaxaca Valley in southern Mexico, centered in their growing city of Monte Alban.

_____ The Maya abandon their cities.

_____ Montezuma II is crowned as the Aztec ruler.

_____ The Olmec develop a civilization; they create giant stone heads.

_____ The Toltecs rule central Mexico.

_____ The Maya build the magnificent city of Tikal.

_____ The Aztecs develop a powerful empire.

6

© 2006 Walch Publishing

People and Regions

Many different peoples lived in the Americas before the Europeans arrived. Match each people listed below with the region where they lived. Write the letter of the region on the line.

_____ 1. Iroquois

_____ 2. Haida

_____ 3. Inca

_____ 4. Cherokee

_____ 5. Cheyenne

_____ 6. Aleut

_____ 7. Aztec

_____ 8. Taina

_____ 9. Pueblo

a. Southeast North America

b. Central America

c. Caribbean

d. Arctic

e. Eastern North America

f. South America

g. Southwest North America

h. Great Plains

i. Northwest Coast

7

© 2006 Walch Publishing

Vocabulary of the Americas

Below are some terms related to the early societies of the
Americas. Write a brief definition of each term.

1. potlach _____

2. pueblo _____

3. sachem _____

4. maize _____

    5. obsidian _____

        6. chinampa _____

            7. quipu _____

8

© 2006 Walch Publishing

North American Cultures

The peoples of North America were very diverse. They had many different cultures and spoke many different languages. Still, their societies shared common elements. Write a check mark next to each cultural trait listed below that was common to most North American societies.

_____ 1. lived in deep harmony with nature

_____ 2. waged war on neighbors constantly

_____ 3 lived by hunting-gathering and/or farming

_____ 4. traded often with other peoples

_____ 5. developed a single, universally understood spoken language

_____ 6. were ruled by a group decision-making process

_____ 7. made religion a part of everyday life

_____ 8. developed a written language

_____ 9. had social units based on family ties

_____ 10. were ruled by a powerful king or emperor

9

© 2006 Walch Publishing

North American Dwellings

The early people of North America lived in a variety of dwellings adapted to their particular environment. Match each people listed below with the description of their typical dwelling. Write the letter of the people on the line.

a. Inuit   b. Plains Indian   c. Hopi   d. Iroquois   e. Kwakiutl

_____ 1. movable tepee made of poles and animal skins

_____ 2. multifamily longhouse made of bark shingles over poles

_____ 3. snug domed shelter made of ice blocks

_____ 4. large rectangular home made of wooden logs and planks

_____ 5. sun-baked clay and stone apartment-style building

10

© 2006 Walch Publishing

Peoples and Regions of North America

Name at least two peoples who lived in each of these areas of North America.

Eastern Woodlands Plains

_____

_____

Northwest Coast

_____

_____

Artic/Subarcic

_____

_____

Southwest

_____

_____

Southeast

_____

_____

11

© 2006 Walch Publishing

Being Anasazi

The Anasazi people lived in what is now the Southwest region of the United States from around 1200 B.C.E. to 1200 C.E. From about 1000 C.E., they lived in large apartment buildings that they built out of rock and adobe (sun-dried clay). At first, their dwellings were on the flat tops of cliffs. Later, the Anasazi moved their dwellings to stone shelves on the sides of these cliffs.

The buildings were often five stories high. Terraces on the flat roofs linked apartments and served as streets. Rooms called kivas were dug into the ground below the apartment buildings. Men met there to discuss group issues and hold religious ceremonies.

To get to their vegetable gardens, the Anasazi had to climb to the top of their cliffs. To get water, they had to climb down to the streams at the bottom of the cliffs. In a year with good rains, basins by the buildings would catch and store water.

Women did the farming. They also made beautifully decorated pottery and finely crafted baskets. Men and older boys hunted and cleared new farm fields.

Imagine you are a member of a cliff-dwelling Anasazi society. Write a paragraph describing a variety of activities you engage in during one day.

12

© 2006 Walch Publishing

African Life

Hundreds of thousands of black Africans arrived in the Americas as slaves during the 1500s. (These numbers would swell to the millions during later centuries.) They were taken mostly from western and central Africa. Circle the answer that best completes each statement below about these Africans' native societies.

1. A major export of the city of Timbuktu in West Africa was

   a. metal goods.   b. books.   c. salt.

2. Many Africans in cities adopted the religion of

   a. Islam.   b. Judaism.   c. Christianity.

3. The first great empire of West Africa was

   a. Songhai.   b. Ghana.   c. Benin.

4. The ruler of the Mali empire who made a famous pilgrimage to Mecca in the Middle East was

   a. Sundiata.   b. Ibn Battuta.   c. Mansa Musa.

5. Children born to slaves in African society were

   a. born free.   b. born as slaves.   c. killed at birth.

13

© 2006 Walch Publishing

Food and Animal Exchanges

The Americas, Europe, and Africa became interconnected during the 1500s. As this happened, new foods and animals were introduced to people who had not known of them before. For each food and animal listed below, write its place of origin on the line.

Americas	Europe	Africa

1. chicken _____

2. potato _____

3. cow _____

4. tomato _____

5. turkey _____

6. black-eyed peas _____

7. lettuce _____

8. coffee bean _____

9. yam _____

10. tobacco _____

11. onions _____

12. banana _____

13. sweet potato _____

14. wheat _____

15. corn _____

16. okra _____

14

© 2006 Walch Publishing

Aztecs, Incas, and Spanish

Hernando Cortés and a force of 600 Spanish soldiers easily vanquished the Aztec empire. Francisco Pizarro and a force of 200 Spanish soldiers easily vanquished the Inca empire. What made these lopsided victories possible? For each factor listed below, write **Spanish** or **Aztecs/Incas** under each heading.

Daily Warm-Ups: U.S. History

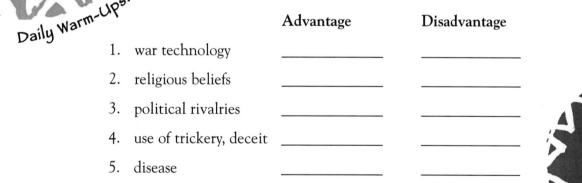

		Advantage	Disadvantage
1.	war technology	_____	_____
2.	religious beliefs	_____	_____
3.	political rivalries	_____	_____
4.	use of trickery, deceit	_____	_____
5.	disease	_____	_____

15

Now, for each factor listed, write one or two sentences explaining why it was an advantage or a disadvantage for the two sides.

© 2006 Walch Publishing

Explorers of the Americas

Christopher Columbus first arrived in the Americas in 1492. Explorers sponsored by various nations of Europe then made their own voyages to the "New World." They claimed the lands they explored for the nation they sailed for.

Record information about some of these early explorations on the chart below. Which of these explorers sailed for a nation that was not his own country? Write the native country of each of these men next to the man's name in the chart.

16

	Nation sailed for	Dates	Where explored
Giovanni Caboto (John Cabot)			
Cristoforo Columbo (Christopher Columbus)		(first voyage)	
Pedro Alvarez Cabral			
Samuel de Champlain			
Henry Hudson			

© 2006 Walch Publishing

Why Explore?

Why were England, France, Spain, and the Netherlands driven to explore and claim parts of the Americas? Some factors are listed below. For each one, write a sentence that tells how that factor motivated European exploration.

1. economics _____

   _____

2. national pride and national rivalries _____

   _____

3. religion _____

   _____

4. technology _____

   _____

17

© 2006 Walch Publishing

Columbus in His Own Words

Cristoforo Columbo, or Christopher Columbus, kept a detailed log (diary) of his voyages. Here are some words he wrote about his first contacts with Amerindians (native peoples) of the Caribbean.

1. *October 24, 1492:* All my world maps and globes strongly suggest that the island of Japan is in this region. I am certain that Cuba and Japan are one and the same.

2. *November 11, 1492:* Beyond doubt this country contains a great amount of gold. It also has precious gems and pearls, and all manner of spices.

3. *December 16, 1492:* These Indians have no weapons and no clothes, and they know nothing about weapons and are very timid. A thousand of them would not stand up to three of our soldiers.

18

Write a sentence below for each quotation that explains what factual mistakes Columbus is making.

1. _____

2. _____

3. _____

© 2006 Walch Publishing

First Settlements

Several different nations of Europe worked to establish a foothold in the Americas. Listed below are the earliest permanent settlements in North America. For each, write the year of founding and the European nation that sponsored the founding.

Settlement	Year	Founding nation
St. Augustine		
Jamestown		
Quebec		
Santa Fe		
Plymouth		
New Amsterdam		

What patterns of settlement do you see in this completed chart? Write one or two sentences for your answer.

19

© 2006 Walch Publishing

New England's Native Americans

The Native American population in the Americas plummeted after Europeans arrived. Here is a graph showing the change in native population in one of the first parts of North America where Europeans set up colonies.

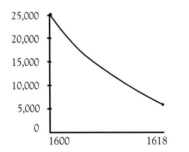

1. Approximately how many Native Americans in New England died between 1600 and 1618? _____

2. The first permanent European settlement in New England was established in 1620. What accounts for the high death toll among New England's Native Americans in the 20 years before 1620?

   _____

   _____

© 2006 Walch Publishing

Daily Warm-Ups: U.S. History

Reasons for Colonies

The European nations that set up colonies in North America had different reasons for doing so. Match each statement to a country in the box. Write the letter of the country on the line. You will use some letters more than once.

a. France	b. Britain	c. Netherlands	d. Spain

_____ 1. Friars set up missions to Christianize native peoples.

_____ 2. Merchants organized expeditions looking for opportunities to make money through trade.

_____ 3. This country established a few settlements to promote its dominant ocean-shipping interests.

_____ 4. Individual conquistadors searched for gold and glory for themselves and for their monarch(s).

_____ 5. Individuals carried on a profitable fur trade while living among the Native Americans.

_____ 6. Later, this country established settlements whose colonists would provide raw materials for trade.

21

© 2006 Walch Publishing

Native American Words

The European colonists adopted a number of Native American words that have remained a part of the English language. Read each definition below. Then write each Native American word in the spaces that follow.

22

1. black and white striped animal; sometimes smelly __ __ __ __ __

2. soft-soled leather shoe __ __ __ __ __ __ __ __

3. vegetable that grows as a vine; is usually green or yellow
   __ __ __ __ __ __

4. long, flat sled without runners __ __ __ __ __ __ __ __

5. large animal; male has enormous, broad antlers __ __ __ __ __

© 2006 Walch Publishing

Views of the Land

Europeans believed in private, individual ownership of land. Each parcel of land had absolute boundaries. Europeans also believed that "unimproved" or "unsettled" land was theirs to claim.

Native Americans had a very different view. Kanekuk, a Kickapoo prophet, explained:

> Some of our chiefs make the claim that the land belongs to us. It is not what the Great Spirit told me. He told me that the lands belong to Him, that no person owns the land; that I was not to forget to tell this to the white people when I met them in council.

Write a paragraph explaining how these two different views caused problems once Europeans started moving into lands where Native Americans lived.

23

© 2006 Walch Publishing

A Tale of Two Colonies

Plymouth and Jamestown were the first two permanent English settlements in North America. Both were settled by people from England. Some things about these settlements, which became the foundations of two colonies, were similar. Other things were different. Label each statement below with a **J** if it applies to Jamestown and/or a **P** if it applies to Plymouth.

_____ 1.   Many colonists died during the first winter.

_____ 2.   Colonists expected and were willing to work hard.

_____ 3.   Governed by a set of rules colonists agreed to among themselves.

_____ 4.   Located in a swampy place with poor drinking water.

_____ 5.   Colonists expected to gather gold with little effort.

_____ 6.   Colonists came to practice their religion in the way they wanted to.

_____ 7.   Relations with Native Americans were usually poor.

24

Views of the Colonies

Colonists who arrived in North America in the early 1600s found a land very unlike the densely populated and cultivated Europe they had left behind. Here are two descriptions of the Cape Cod Bay area of Massachusetts written by soon-to-be colonists.

"A hideous and desolate wilderness, full of wild beasts and wild men."

"Pleasant of air and prospect [appearance], with much plenty both of fish and fowl."

What do you think might account for such very different reactions? Write a paragraph to answer this question.

25

© 2006 Walch Publishing

Colonial Regions

The early North American colonies are classified into three regions. Those regions are listed below. Under each heading, name at least three colonies that were part of that region.

New England

_____

_____

_____

Middle Colonies

_____

_____

_____

Southern Colonies

_____

_____

_____

For each region, write a sentence that describes the main characteristics of that region.

© 2006 Walch Publishing

Colony Names

England set up a number of colonies along North America's eastern seaboard. For each colony listed below, write the origin of its name on the line.

1. Massachusetts _____

2. Virginia _____

3. Delaware _____

4. Carolinas _____

5. Connecticut _____

6. New York _____

7. New Jersey _____

8. Maryland _____

9. Pennsylvania _____

27

© 2006 Walch Publishing

Early Colonial Events

Listed below are significant events in the North American colonies during the 1600s. Number them from 1 to 8 in the order in which they happened, with 1 being the earliest event.

_____ King Philip's War rages.

_____ First cargo of African-American slaves lands in Virginia.

_____ Harvard College is founded.

_____ England enacts the first of the Navigation Acts.

_____ John Rolfe introduces West Indian tobacco to Virginia.

_____ Bacon's Rebellion takes place.

_____ Roger Williams gets a charter for Rhode Island.

_____ New Netherland becomes New York.

28

© 2006 Walch Publishing

An Appeal for Colonists

A 1681 London pamphlet advertised Pennsylvania as a place where men who

> . . . could not only not marry in England, but hardly live and allow themselves clothes, do marry in Pennsylvania, and bestow thrice [three times as much] in all necessities and conveniences for themselves, their wives and children, both as to apparel and household goods.

What types of people in England do you think this advertisement would appeal to? Consider both women's and men's reactions to the advertisement. Then write a paragraph as your answer.

29

© 2006 Walch Publishing

Seeds of Democracy

Democracy started early in the North American colonies. Agreements were written and law-making bodies were formed. These allowed (male) colonists to be in charge of some of their colony's affairs. They provided some individual personal rights.

Match each agreement or law-making body below with the colony or settlement it applies to. Write the letter of the colony on the line.

_____ 1. Mayflower Compact

_____ 2. House of Burgesses

_____ 3. Concessions and Agreements

_____ 4. Fundamental Orders

_____ 5. Frame of Government

_____ 6. General Court

a. New Jersey

b. Massachusetts

c. Virginia

d. Connecticut

e. Plymouth

f. Pennsylvania

30

© 2006 Walch Publishing

Religious Motives

Religion was often a factor that motivated people to come to the North American colonies. Identify the religious group that matches each description. Then write the correct religious group on the line.

Catholics	Huguenots	Quakers
Pilgrims	Jews	Mennonites

1. came to Pennsylvania to escape persecution in Germany
   _____

2. came to Massachusetts to get away from Church of England rituals and practices _____

3. came to Maryland, a colony set up to provide a haven for them
   _____

4. came to Pennsylvania to escape persecution in England
   _____

5. came from France to escape persecution there _____

6. came from Portugal and Spain to escape persecution there
   _____

31

© 2006 Walch Publishing

Colonial Women

The women named in the box below were well-known during their lifetimes in colonial North America. Match each woman with her description. Write the letter of the correct woman on the line.

a. Eliza Lucas	c. Silence Dogood	e. Mary Dyer
b. Anne Bradstreet	d. Dinah Nuthead	f. Margaret Brent

____1. middle-aged widow whose funny and satiric letters were published in the *New England Courant*

____2. wealthy plantation owner who acted as Lord Baltimore's lawyer

____3. operated a printing press in Annapolis, Maryland, in the 1690s

____4. managed South Carolina plantations as a teenager and developed indigo as a profitable crop

____5. hanged in Boston in 1660 for refusing to obey the law banishing Quakers

____6. renowned Puritan poet whose work was published in 1650

One of these women was not a real person. Which one is it? Who was "she"?

32

© 2006 Walch Publishing

Colonial Workers

The colonial economy was always in need of workers. The population in the colonies was small, so a lot of new workers had to come from Europe. Several types of people supplied this labor. These are listed in the box below. Write which type of worker each of the following statements applies to.

indentured servant	free immigrant
transported convict	slave

1. You are bound to your master for seven years. _____

2. You must work for your master for no pay for all of your life. _____

3. You may be free on arrival in the colonies, or you may have to sign with a master for an agreed number of years. _____

4. You can engage in the economic activity of your choice. _____

5. Your master must provide clothing, tools, and other benefits when your term of service ends. _____

6. Your children are bound to your master as you are. _____

33

© 2006 Walch Publishing

Indentured Servants

The life of an indentured servant was entirely determined by her or his master. A master was required to provide food, lodging, and clothing to the servant. But how much and of what quality to provide was up to the master. Lyrics from a ditty titled "The Lads of Virginia" express an indentured servant's dismay:

34

When I was in England
I could live at my ease,
Rest my bones down on soft leathers,
my hand
And a lass on my knee,
I thought myself fit for all weathers.

But now in Virginia I lay like a dog,
Our pillow at night is a brick or a log
We dress and undressWith a jug in
Like some other sea hog,
How hard is our fate in Virginia. . . .
If ever I live to see
Seven years more,

Imagine you are an indentured servant in an American colony. Describe the drawbacks of your position.

© 2006 Walch Publishing

Tobacco

King James I of England described the smoking of tobacco as "a custom loathsome to the eye, hateful to the nose, harmful to the brain, [and] dangerous to the lung." Yet tobacco growing was a key factor in the development of the Virginia colony.

Write one or two sentences to answer each of the following questions.

1. Why did Virginia colonists eagerly turn to tobacco growing?

   _____

   _____

   _____

2. How did tobacco agriculture change the labor system in Virginia?

   _____

   _____

   _____

35

© 2006 Walch Publishing

African and American Slavery

Slavery had been a part of African society for many centuries. The conditions of African slavery were different from American slavery. Write a check mark next to each statement below that is true of African, as opposed to American, slavery.

____ 1. One would become a slave when captured as a prisoner of war.

____ 2. Children were born slaves.

____ 3. A slave became a member of the slave-owning family.

____ 4. Slaves could become free through marriage.

____ 5. As a field hand, slaves had little contact with slave owners.

____ 6. A slave was a slave for life.

____ 7. A slave could purchase his or her own freedom.

36

© 2006 Walch Publishing

African Words

African slaves brought African words with them that have become a part of the English language. Write each African-American word in the spaces after its definition.

1. a slightly curved fruit with a yellow or red skin

    — — — — — —

2. a thick, okra-based soup

    — — — — —

3. a musical instrument with a round body, long neck, and five strings

    — — — — —

4. a small, tree-dwelling African ape

    — — — — — — — — —

5. a tropical plant with an edible starchy tuber

    — — —

6. a religion practiced today mainly in Haiti

    — — — — — —

37

© 2006 Walch Publishing

Earning a Living

Colonists all through North America pursued many of the same economic activities. But some economic activities were most often found in certain regions. For each description below, name a colony where you most likely live.

1. You build ships from lumber harvested in your region.
   _____

2. You operate a large and prosperous wheat farm.
   _____

3. You oversee a sprawling tobacco plantation. _____

4. You operate an iron-producing business. _____

5. You earn your living by fishing and, later, whaling. _____

6. You operate a rice plantation. _____

7. You create rum from molasses. _____

38

© 2006 Walch Publishing

Rebellions and Revolts

Life was not always tranquil in the colonies. Frontier settlers and militia leaders led some rebellions. African-American slaves revolted, too. Circle the letter of the rebellion that each of the following sentences describes.

1. Small farmers in western Virginia burned the capital at Jamestown.

   a. Bacon's Rebellion   b. Leisler's Rebellion

2. Slaves attacked whites in South Carolina and then fled toward Florida.

   a. Nat Turner's Revolt   b. Stono Rebellion

3. A New York militia leader seized control of New York's government.

   a. Stono Rebellion   b. Leisler's Rebellion

4. Frontier settlers in Pennsylvania massacred a village of peaceful Indians.

   a. Paxton Boys' Uprising   b. Annapolis Uprising

5. Slaves set a fire in a major city and then, as planned, killed whites who gathered to put it out.

   a. Shays' Rebellion   b. New York City Revolt

39

© 2006 Walch Publishing

Triangular Trade

A "triangular trade" developed along sea routes that linked **North America, Europe, Africa,** and the **Caribbean** region. Next to each trade item listed below, write the region it was shipped to. Use the four regions listed above. Some items may have been shipped to more than one region.

1. manufactured goods _____

2. rum _____

3. slaves _____

4. furs _____

5. fruit _____

6. textiles _____

7. iron _____

8. flour _____

9. sugar _____

10. lumber _____

11. molasses _____

12. tobacco _____

13. fish _____

14. gunpowder _____

40

© 2006 Walch Publishing

Population Charts

The first U.S. census, taken in 1790, showed the European origins of the white population for each state or colony. The pie charts below show the national origins of the populations of Massachusetts and Pennsylvania as recorded in that census.

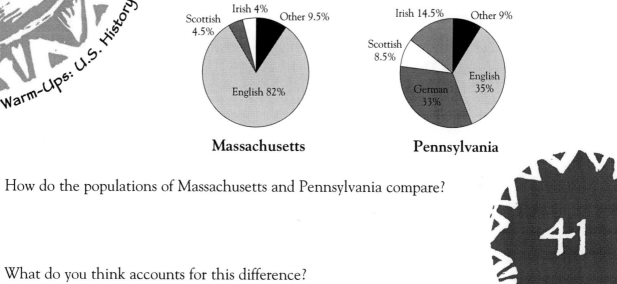

Massachusetts

Pennsylvania

1. How do the populations of Massachusetts and Pennsylvania compare?

2. What do you think accounts for this difference?

41

© 2006 Walch Publishing

The Navigation Acts

The British Parliament passed the Navigation Acts in the 1650s. These laws regulated colonial trade to benefit England, the mother country. Check each type of trade described below that was allowed under the Navigation Acts.

_____ 1.   A planter ships his tobacco from North Carolina to Spain.

_____ 2.   A New York merchant sends beaver pelts to Scotland.

_____ 3.   A Dutch ship transports salted cod from
Massachusetts to the British West Indies.

_____ 4.   A Spanish ship sends wine to England, where the wine is loaded onto
a British ship that takes it to Pennsylvania.

_____ 5.   A Rhode Island ship brings molasses to British importers in London.

_____ 6.   A Portuguese ship unloads half of its cargo of fruit in London, then sails
to Maryland with the rest of the fruit.

42

In a sentence for each trading venture described above, explain why the venture
did or did not comply with the Navigation Acts.

© 2006 Walch Publishing

British v. French

Beginning in the late 1600s, Britain and France fought a series of wars. The conflicts spread from Europe to North America, where colonists became involved. Each of these wars affected North American colonists—sometimes in a positive way, sometimes not.

The four British-French wars in the colonies are listed below. For each, tell in a sentence its positive, negative, or neutral effect on England's North American colonists.

1. King William's War (1689–1697) _____

_____

2. Queen Anne's War (1702–1713) _____

_____

3. King George's War (1740–1748) _____

_____

4. French and Indian War (1754–1763) _____

_____

43

© 2006 Walch Publishing

British Colonial Laws

Carrying on the French and Indian (Seven Years') War was very expensive. After the war ended in 1763, Britain decided its American colonies should help pay those costs. So Britain passed a series of laws to raise more money from the colonies and take tighter control of them.

Match each law listed in the box with its description below. Write the letter of the law on the line.

a. Writs of Assistance	c. Stamp Act	e. Sugar Act
b. Townshend Acts	d. Quartering Act	

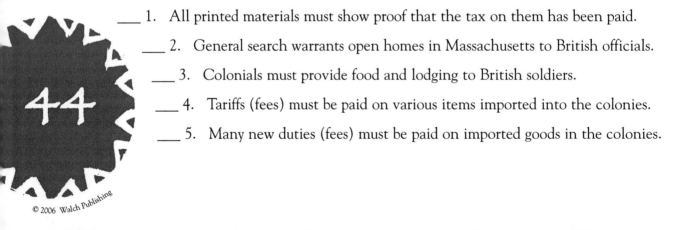

____ 1. All printed materials must show proof that the tax on them has been paid.

____ 2. General search warrants open homes in Massachusetts to British officials.

____ 3. Colonials must provide food and lodging to British soldiers.

____ 4. Tariffs (fees) must be paid on various items imported into the colonies.

____ 5. Many new duties (fees) must be paid on imported goods in the colonies.

44

© 2006 Walch Publishing

Actions and Reactions

Britain's new laws sparked outrage among the colonists. An escalating series of British actions and colonial reactions almost inevitably drew the two sides into war. Number each event of this series from 1 to 10, with 1 being the earliest event. (*Hint:* Keep in mind the action-reaction-action-reaction nature of events.)

_____ British troops are sent into Boston.

_____ The British close Boston Harbor.

_____ Colonists meet in the Stamp Act Congress.

_____ The Boston Tea Party takes place.

_____ The Boston Massacre happens.

_____ The Stamp Act is passed.

_____ The First Continental Congress meets.

_____ The Tea Act is passed.

45

© 2006 Walch Publishing

Colonists: British or American?

John Rutledge of South Carolina was a leading figure in South Carolina politics. He had studied to become a lawyer in London, England's capital city. In 1765 at age 26, Rutledge sailed to New York City from South Carolina to attend the Stamp Act Congress. He wrote to his mother after he arrived in New York, "It is my first trip to a foreign country."

Rutledge had spent some years in England. Why did he say in his letter from New York City that he was visiting "a foreign country" for the first time? What does this tell us about the sense of national identity among the colonists? Write a paragraph as your answer.

46

© 2006 Walch Publishing

The Declaration of Independence

The men meeting at the Second Continental Congress approved the Declaration of Independence on July 4, 1776. After a one-paragraph preamble, the Declaration says:

We hold these truths to be self-evident, that all men are created equal, that they are endowed by their Creator with certain unalienable Rights, that among these are Life, Liberty and the pursuit of Happiness. That to secure these rights, Governments are instituted among Men, deriving their just powers from the consent of the governed, that whenever any Form of Government becomes destructive of these ends, it is the Right of the People to alter or to abolish it, and to institute new Government, laying foundation on such principles and organizing its powers in such form, as to them shall seem most likely to effect their Safety and Happiness.

1. What four principles does the Declaration declare in these two sentences?

2. What people do you think the Declaration refers to when it says "all men are created equal"? Explain your reasoning.

47

© 2006 Walch Publishing

Americans v. British

When the Revolutionary War began, most people would have said that the British had most advantages. But some disadvantages worked against them. The Americans, too, enjoyed advantages and were burdened by disadvantages. For each statement below, write which side it applies to—American or British—and whether it was an advantage or a disadvantage.

1. It is an industrial nation. _____

2. The war is fought on its home turf. _____

3. It has little money to support its army. _____

4. Its citizen-soldiers come and go. _____

5. Its home base is across the ocean. _____

6. It has a trained, professional army. _____

7. It has a good commander-in-chief. _____

8. Its leaders are inefficient and not well qualified. _____

48

© 2006 Walch Publishing

George Washington

George Washington was born in 1732 in Virginia and grew up on his parents' tobacco plantations there. He often visited the home of his sister-in-law's family, which was part of the colonial elite. Washington learned the social graces as he grew into a 6-foot 2-inch robust young man.

At age 16, he was part of a surveying party that probed the unsettled lands just to the west. At age 17, he became the official surveyor of Culpepper County, Virginia. The governor of Virginia sent him west at age 21 to tell the French at Fort Duquesne (today's Pittsburgh) that they were trespassing on Virginia territory.

At age 23, Washington was commander of the Virginia army along the Indian frontier. He and his troops fought alongside General Braddock's forces at Fort Duquesne. There, Washington saw that the French and Indian guerrilla tactics could defeat the traditional British style of "orderly" battle. Braddock died in that battle. George Washington escaped with four bullet holes in his coat.

Can you see why George Washington's background made him an excellent choice as commander-in-chief of the Continental (American) army? Write a paragraph as your answer.

49

© 2006 Walch Publishing

Revolutionary Words

Even today we remember some memorable statements made by Revolutionary-era people. Match each statement with the person who said it. Write the letter of the person on the line.

a. Thomas Paine	c. John Parker	e. John Paul Jones
b. Patrick Henry	d. Samuel Adams	

_____ 1. If this be treason, make the most of it.

_____ 2. These are the times that try men's souls.

_____ 3. I have not yet begun to fight.

_____ 4. Mankind are governed more by their feelings than by reason.

_____ 5. Don't fire unless fired upon. But if they mean to have a war, let it begin here.

50

© 2006 Walch Publishing

Early Battles of the Revolution

Some early battles and engagements of the Revolutionary War were very significant. For each event listed below, give the date and explain its importance.

1. Lexington and Concord _____

_____

2. Bunker (Breed's) Hill _____

_____

3. Fort Ticonderoga _____

_____

4. Long Island and New York _____

_____

5. Trenton _____

_____

51

© 2006 Walch Publishing

Revolutionary Women

Women played many roles in the Revolutionary era. Match each woman listed below with her description. Write the letter of the description on the line.

_____ 1. Mary Brant   a. playwright, historian

_____ 2. Margaret Corbin   b. poet, slave

_____ 3. Phillis Wheatley   c. Mohawk Indian leader

_____ 4. Mercy Otis Warren   d. printer

_____ 5. Mary Katherine Goddard   e. Continental army cannoneer

52

© 2006 Walch Publishing

Benjamin Franklin

Benjamin Franklin was a remarkable person. He achieved many accomplishments in many fields. Write a check mark for each accomplishment listed below that applies to Franklin.

_____ 1. created the American postal system

_____ 2. measured the Gulf Stream

_____ 3. invented the Franklin stove

_____ 4. introduced spaghetti to America

_____ 5. founded a library

_____ 6. designed the University of Virginia

_____ 7. invented bifocal lenses for glasses

_____ 8. wrote the Declaration of Independence

_____ 9. made scientific discoveries about electricity

_____ 10. published a very popular almanac

_____ 11. founded the University of Pennsylvania

_____ 12. invented the lightning rod

53

© 2006 Walch Publishing

War Propaganda

Paul Revere created and sold a color engraving of the Boston Massacre that is famous. He titled it *The Bloody Massacre Perpetrated in King Street*. Below the picture of British soldiers firing on unarmed Boston men was a poem. The first stanza of that poem reads as follows:

Unhappy Boston! see thy sons deplore, Thy hallow'd Walks besmear'd with guiltless Gore. While faithless P____n and his savage Bands, With murd'rous Rancour stretch their bloody hands, Like fierce Barbarians grinning o'er their Prey, Approve the Carnage and enjoy the Day.

54

These lines of poetry are an example of propaganda. Explain in a paragraph why it is accurate to label these words as propaganda.

© 2006 Walch Publishing

African Americans

African Americans played important roles in the Revolutionary and post-Revolutionary era. Match each person in the box with her or his description below. Write the correct letter on the line.

a. James Forten	c. Benjamin Banneker	e. Richard Allen or Absalom Jones
b. Lucy Prince Terry	d. Peter Salem	

_____ 1. fought at Lexington and Bunker Hill

_____ 2. a skilled astronomer who published almanacs

_____ 3. slave and poet who argued a case before the U.S. Supreme Court

_____ 4. wealthy owner of a large sailmaking business

_____ 5. organized the Free African Society in Philadelphia

55

© 2006 Walch Publishing

Native Americans

Events of the Revolutionary era affected Native Americans, usually in negative ways. Each statement below is about an event that involved Native Americans. Label each statement **T** if it is entirely true or **F** if it is false in any way. (All dates are correct.) Rewrite any false statements to make them true.

_____ 1. Iroquois allied with Tories carried out the Wyoming Valley massacre in 1778.

_____ 2. The Proclamation of 1763 opened the western frontier to white settlers.

_____ 3. Lord Dunsmore's War defeated the Shawnee in 1774.

_____ 4. In each Treaty of Fort Stanwix, the Iroquois gave up lands to the French.

_____ 5. The Cherokee signed the Treaty of Hopewell in 1785.

_____ 6. Sullivan's Campaign of 1778–1779 was aimed against the Delaware and Miami.

56

© 2006 Walch Publishing

The Articles of Confederation

The Articles of Confederation set up the new national government. Some powers were left to the states. Other powers were given to the national government. Write **S** next to each power described below that remained with the states. Write **N** next to each power that the Articles gave to the national government.

_____ 1. issue money

_____ 2. declare war

_____ 3. maintain a militia

_____ 4. form an army

_____ 5. collect taxes

_____ 6. regulate Native American affairs

_____ 7. make rules of trade

_____ 8. enforce laws

_____ 9. set up a postal service

_____ 10. conduct foreign affairs

57

© 2006 Walch Publishing

Constitutional Words

Each word below relates to the U.S. Constitution and the process of creating it. Write the correct word from the box to complete each sentence below. You will not use every word.

amendment	ratify	preamble
confederation	compromise	veto

1. The Constitution begins with a(n) _____.

2. The Constitution can be changed by adding a(n) _____ to it.

3. The delegates had to agree to more than one _____ in order to reach agreement.

4. Before the Constitution went into effect, the states had to _____ it.

58

© 2006 Walch Publishing

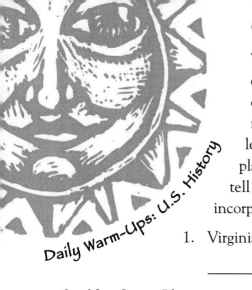

Compromise and the Constitution

The men who met to draw up the U.S. Constitution had many different opinions. They had to agree to some compromises in order to get their job done. One of the biggest issues was how many representatives (lawmakers) each state would have in the legislature (the law-making branch of the government). Three plans were proposed. Write a sentence describing each plan. Also, tell which states supported each plan. Then tell which plan was incorporated into the Constitution.

1. Virginia Plan _____

   _____

2. New Jersey Plan _____

   _____

3. Connecticut Plan _____

   _____

Plan chosen: _____

59

© 2006 Walch Publishing

The Branches of Government

The U.S. Constitution divides the federal government into three distinct branches. Write an **L** next to each power below that applies to the legislative branch. Write an **E** next to each power that applies to the executive branch. Write a **J** next to each power that applies to the judicial branch.

_____ 1. makes treaties

_____ 2. sets and collects taxes

_____ 3. maintains armies

_____ 4. commands the armed forces

_____ 5. hears and decides legal cases

_____ 6. carries out laws

_____ 7. declares war

_____ 8. passes laws

_____ 9. conducts impeachments

_____ 10. appoints Supreme Court judges

60

© 2006 Walch Publishing

Daily Warm-Ups: U.S. History

Slavery and the Constitution

The framers of the Constitution wrestled with the issue of slavery. In the end, they reached several compromises about slavery. Look at a copy of the U.S. Constitution. Find these compromises dealing with slavery, and describe each one in a sentence.

1. the slave trade

_____

_____

_____

2. counting population for voting and taxing purposes

_____

_____

_____

What do you think about these compromises? Are they fair? Should they have been made? Write your opinion in a paragraph that explains your reasoning.

61

© 2006 Walch Publishing

More Constitutional Words

Each word in the box relates to a provision in the U.S. Constitution. Write the correct word from the box after each definition below. You will not use every word.

| electoral college | Senate | representative |
| majority | impeachment | veto |

1. bringing formal charges of wrongdoing against a public official
   _____

2. more than half of something _____

3. a person who is chosen to speak or act for others _____

4. the power to stop the passing of a law _____

5. the body of voters that elects the president and vice president of the United States _____

© 2006 Walch Publishing

Daily Warm-Ups: U.S. History

The Bill of Rights

The Bill of Rights is not an actual bill, or law. It is much more important than that. It is the first ten amendments to the U.S. Constitution. They were added to the Constitution very quickly, to protect individual rights. Do you know which of your own rights the Bill of Rights protects? Write those rights on the lines after each amendment below.

Amendment 1: _____

_____

Amendment 2: _____

_____

Amendment 4: _____

_____

Amendment 6: _____

_____

63

© 2006 Walch Publishing

Federalists and Anti-Federalists

The question of whether or not to ratify the Constitution was widely debated all over the country. People who favored it were called **Federalists.** People who opposed it were called **Anti-Federalists.** Read each quotation below. Write **F** next to each one that was spoken by a Federalist. Write **AF** next to each one that was spoken by an Anti-Federalist.

_____ 1. "Those who own the country ought to run it."

_____ 2. "The Constitution is horribly frightful. It squints toward monarchy."

_____ 3. "The people are turbulent and changing; they seldom judge or determine right. Give therefore to the first class a distinct, permanent share of the government."

_____ 4. "I am not among those who fear the people. They and not the rich are our dependence for continued freedom."

Bonus: Conduct some research, and find out who made each of these statements.

64

© 2006 Walch Publishing

The New Nation

Each word in the box relates to events of the late 1700s and early 1800s. Match each word with its definition below. You will not use every word. Write the letter of the word on the line.

a. alien	c. sedition	e. neutral
b. federal	d. cabinet	f. tariff

_____ 1. a set of taxes on imported goods

_____ 2. a person living in one country who was born in a different country and remains a citizen of a foreign country

_____ 3. promoting resistance to or rebellion against lawful authority

_____ 4. a group of people who advise the head of a nation

_____ 5. not taking one side or the other in a fight or argument

65

© 2006 Walch Publishing

Citizens' Rebellions

Two rebellions erupted in the new nation—**Shays' Rebellion** (1786–1787) and the **Whiskey Rebellion** (1794). They were alike in many ways. Write **S** and/or **W** next to each element listed below, according to which rebellion it applies to. Some elements apply to both rebellions.

_____ 1. This protested taxes on farmers.

_____ 2. Protestors marched on the state capital.

_____ 3. The state militia put down the rebellion.

_____ 4. Debtors lost their farms and were jailed.

_____ 5. Western farmers opposed eastern money powers.

_____ 6. Mobs disrupted law and order.

_____ 7. This took place in Pennsylvania.

_____ 8. This took place in Massachusetts.

66

© 2006 Walch Publishing

Supreme Court Cases

The U.S. Supreme Court, headed by Chief Justice John Marshall, made some very important decisions in the early 1800s. They established the Supreme Court as a powerful branch of the federal government. Match each case named below with the correct ruling. Write the letter of the correct decision on the line.

_____ 1. *Marbury v. Madison*

_____ 2. *McCulloch v. Maryland*

_____ 3. *Fletcher v. Peck*

a. The Supreme Court can strike down a state law that conflicts with a federal law.

b. The Supreme Court can reverse a president's veto of a constitutional law.

c. The Supreme Court can strike down laws passed by the U.S. Congress that it decides are in violation of the U.S. Constitution.

d. The Supreme Court can strike down state laws that it decides are in violation of the U.S. Constitution.

67

© 2006 Walch Publishing

The Alien and Sedition Acts

In 1798, Federalists in Congress passed oppressive laws known as the Alien and Sedition Acts, intended to silence their Republican opponents. Below is part of the Sedition Act:

> That if any person shall write, print, utter, or publish . . . any false, scandalous and malicious writing or writings against the government of the United States, or either house of the Congress of the United States, or the President of the United States, with intent to . . . bring them into contempt or disrepute, or to . . . oppose or resist any law of the United States . . . then such person [if legally convicted] . . . shall be punished by a fine . . . and by imprisonment.

1. Which freedoms guaranteed by the Bill of Rights does this law perhaps violate?

   _____

2. Which constitutional amendment protects these freedoms?

   _____

3. Do you think this law goes against the Constitution? Write your answer in a paragraph that explains your reasoning.

68

© 2006 Walch Publishing

Political Nicknames

Nicknames quickly attached themselves to men who campaigned to be U.S. president in the 1800s. Match each politician listed below with his popular nickname. Write the letter of the correct nickname on the line.

a.	Old Tippecanoe	e.	the Great Pacificator
b.	Old Rough and Ready	f.	Old Kinderhook
c.	His Accidency	g.	Young Hickory
d.	Old Hickory	h.	Old Fuss and Feathers

____ 1. Martin Van Buren

____ 2. Andrew Jackson

____ 3. James Polk

____ 4. William Henry Harrison

____ 5. Winfield Scott

____ 6. Zachary Taylor

____ 7. Henry Clay

____ 8. John Tyler

69

For each man named above, explain in a sentence why he earned that nickname.

© 2006 Walch Publishing

Campaign Slogans

Slogans attached to political campaigns emerged in the first part of the 1800s. For each of the following slogans, explain in a sentence what appeal to voters the slogan makes.

1. Fifty-four forty or fight. _____

_____

_____

2. Tippecanoe and Tyler too. _____

_____

_____

3. Free soil, free men, free speech, free labor, Frémont. _____

_____

_____

70

© 2006 Walch Publishing

Campaign Songs

Political campaigns in the 1800s were lively and contentious. Campaign songs were very popular, and sometimes quite insulting. The lyrics below are from an 1828 song titled "The Hickory Tree."

> While Jonny was lounging on crimson and down,
>
> And stuffing both pockets with pelf,
>
> Brave Andrew was pulling John Bull's colors down,
>
> And paying his army himself.

Who is Jonny? Who is Andrew? Who is John Bull? What are "crimson and down" and "pelf"? Which army is the song referring to? Explain the lyrics and the song's title in your own words.

71

© 2006 Walch Publishing

Manifest Destiny

A New York newspaper writer named John L. O'Sullivan insisted that the United States was intended to spread all the way west across the continent to the Pacific Ocean. Here is what he said about this:

> [It is] our **manifest destiny** to overspread the continent allotted by Providence for the free development of our yearly multiplying millions.

What do you think of this statement? Was the United States inevitably going to take over the lands from the Atlantic to the Pacific, across the continent? What forces might have "destined" (fated) it to do so? What forces might have prevented it from doing so? Write a paragraph as your answer.

© 2006 Walch Publishing

The New Lands

The national government sponsored an exploring expedition in 1820 to find out more about the new national lands. U.S. Army Major Stephen H. Long led the expedition. Read part of his report below. Then answer the questions that follow.

> In regard to this extensive section of the country, I do not hesitate in giving the opinion, that it is almost wholly unfit for cultivation, and of course, uninhabitable by a people depending upon agriculture for their subsistence.

1. What part of the nation do you think Long is describing?

    _____

    _____

2. How accurate or inaccurate was Long's description, as revealed by later developments in that region?

    _____

    _____

73

© 2006 Walch Publishing

The Westward Journey

Pioneers started off from St. Louis, Missouri, in wagon trains headed to the West Coast, on the Pacific Ocean end of the nation. They traveled in covered wagons pulled by oxen. All of a family's supplies and possessions were in their wagon.

The trip from Missouri to the West Coast was about 2,000 miles. Most wagon trains could travel about 15 miles per day. How many days would this take?

2,000 miles ÷ 15 miles per day = _____ days

_____ days = _____ months

74

Many days did not yield 15 miles of progress. Delays were common. What problems along the trip were very likely to cause delays? List them, or describe them in a paragraph.

© 2006 Walch Publishing

Notable Women

Four notable women of the mid-1800s are described below. Read each description. Then answer the question for each: Who was I?

1. My slave name was Isabella. I ran away to New York and freedom. There, I chose a new name for myself. It described my new life of traveling and speaking out about the realities of slavery. Who was I?

   _____

2. I was chubby and merry, and happily married. I had seven children and was a housewife. I also was a founder of the women's rights movement and a principal organizer of the Seneca Falls Convention. Who was I? _____

3. I was small, and I looked frail, but I had seven children. I wrote a hugely popular novel that caused President Lincoln to call me "the little lady who made this big war." Who was I?

   _____

4. I wanted to go to college, but no colleges accepted women students. So I founded the first U.S. college for women, in Massachusetts. Who was I?

   _____

75

© 2006 Walch Publishing

Women's Status

Women of the nineteenth century led very restrictive lives. They had few rights. Write **T** next to each statement below about women's rights in the 1800s that is true. Write **F** next to each statement that is false in any way.

_____ 1. She is paid the same as a man for doing the same job.

_____ 2. The money she earns belongs to her husband.

_____ 3. She can attend state colleges but not private colleges.

_____ 4. She cannot vote, so she has no way to change laws.

_____ 5. Her husband can legally beat or whip her.

_____ 6. She keeps her own property when she gets married.

_____ 7. She is scorned and shunned by society if she gets a divorce.

_____ 8. If she leaves her husband, she usually gets custody of the children.

_____ 9. The Constitution guarantees her equal rights with men.

_____ 10. She cannot serve on a jury, and often she cannot testify in court.

76

© 2006 Walch Publishing

Words of the 1800s

The words in the box relate to issues and policies of the first half of the 1800s. Use a word from the box to complete each sentence. You will not use all the words.

assimilation	tariff	manifest destiny
impressment	embargo	proviso

1. _____ was the belief that the United States was fated to expand westward across the continent.

2. One cause of the War of 1812 was the British practice of _____, seizing sailors from U.S. ships.

3. A(n) _____ law of 1807 banned all exports from U.S. ports.

4. Northern businesses mostly favored a(n) _____ (a fee on imports), while southerners mostly opposed this.

5. In the early 1800s, the U.S. government favored _____ of Native Americans rather than removal.

77

© 2006 Walch Publishing

Words to Remember

Politicians, reformers, inventors—all had memorable things to say in the mid-1800s. Match each statement with the person who said or wrote it. Write the correct letter on the line.

a. Daniel Webster	c. Henry Clay
b. Samuel F. B. Morse	d. William Lloyd Garrison

_____ 1. "I had rather be right than be president."

_____ 2. "Liberty and Union, now and forever, one and inseparable."

_____ 3. "I do not wish to think, or speak, or write with moderation. No! no!"

_____ 4. "What hath God wrought?"

78

© 2006 Walch Publishing

Slave Revolts

Several slave revolts greatly alarmed Southern whites in the years before the Civil War. Write one or two sentences that give the details about each revolt led by the person named below.

1. Gabriel Prosser _____

_____

_____

2. Denmark Vesey_____

_____

_____

3. Nat Turner _____

_____

_____

79

© 2006 Walch Publishing

Hidden Messages

African-American slaves created songs called spirituals. These seemed to be about Christian beliefs and Bible stories. But often the lyrics expressed hidden hopes and messages about escape from the South and slavery. Read these lyrics from the beautiful spiritual "Swing Low, Sweet Chariot."

I looked over Jordan, _____

And what did I see? _____

Comin' for to carry me home. _____

80

A band of angels _____

Comin' after me, _____

Comin' for to carry me home. _____

What hidden meanings do you find in these lyrics? Write each one on the line next to that lyric.

© 2006 Walch Publishing

Escape or Stay?

African-American slaves, of course, yearned for freedom. But escape was very dangerous. Capture carried dire consequences. Imagine you are a slave whose master treats you well, by the standards of Southern slavery. You think a lot about escaping, but you have your doubts.

Under "Reasons to go," list at least three reasons to attempt to escape. Under "Reasons to stay," list at least three reasons to stay on the plantation. After reviewing your reasons, what is your decision? Will you stay or will you go?

Reasons to go	Reasons to stay

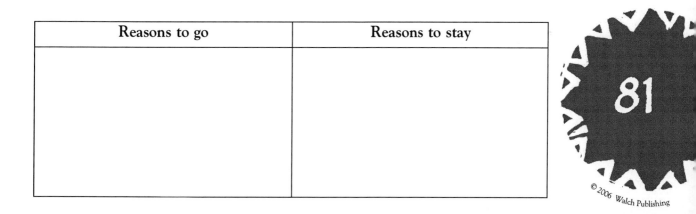

81

© 2006 Walch Publishing

Technology and Change

Advances in technology can propel significant economic and social changes. Number each development below 1 through 7 in the order that it occurred in time, with 1 being the earliest. It will help you to answer if you keep in mind the cause-and-effect cycle of advance and change.

_____ Eli Whitney invents the "cotton engine."

_____ Selling cotton to textile manufacturers becomes much more profitable.

_____ Mechanical looms create mass manufacture of cotton cloth.

_____ Cotton processing becomes much less expensive.

_____ Slavery expands tremendously throughout the lower South.

_____ Demand for cotton increases rapidly.

_____ Cotton farming expands widely through the lower South.

82

© 2006 Walch Publishing

The Transportation Revolution

Improvements in transportation systems were a big factor in the growth of the U.S. economy in the 1800s. Number these developments in transportation in the order in which they occurred with number 1 being the earliest.

_____ The Erie Canal opens, leading a boom in canal building.

_____ Steam-powered ships take over cross-Atlantic transportation.

_____ Railroads take the place of many canals and turnpikes.

_____ The stagecoach transports most travelers on challenging roads.

_____ Construction of the National Road begins in Maryland.

_____ Fast-sailing clipper ships become the fastest type of sea-route transportation.

_____ John Fitch begins operating the first regularly scheduled steamboat.

83

© 2006 Walch Publishing

Native American Losses

Native Americans of the eastern United States suffered devastating setbacks in the first half of the 1800s. Describe each battle listed below. Then write a sentence that tells the significance of the battle to the Native Americans involved.

1. Battle of Tippecanoe _____
   _____
   _____

2. Battle of Horseshoe Bend _____
   _____
   _____

   3. First Seminole War _____
      _____
      _____

   4. Second Seminole War _____
      _____
      _____

84

© 2006 Walch Publishing

Tecumseh's Plan

The Shawnee leader Tecumseh traveled all through the eastern United States in the 1800s. He ranged from the Wisconsin country to Florida. He visited tribe after tribe.

His aim was to gather all the eastern tribes to join in one great confederation so they could resist the whites and push them off native lands. At each stop, Tecumseh used his powerful speaking skills to persuade each tribe to join with him. These are some of his words:

Where today are the Pequot? Where are the Narragansett, the Mohican, the Pokanoket, and many other once powerful tribes of our people? They have vanished before the greed and the oppression of the White Man, as snow before a summer sun.

Will we let ourselves be destroyed in our turn without a struggle, give up our homes, our country bequeathed to us by the Great Spirit, the graves of our dead and everything that is dear to us? I know you will cry with me, "Never! Never!"

Imagine that Tecumseh is making an appeal to your Native American tribe. What do you think? Will you vote to join Tecumseh's union or will you vote to keep out of it? Explain your decision and your reasoning in a paragraph.

85

© 2006 Walch Publishing

Worcester v. Georgia

In 1832, the U.S. Supreme Court decided a case titled *Worcester v. Georgia*. The Court ruled that the Cherokee were "a distinct community occupying their own territory in which the laws of Georgia can have no force."

Georgia ignored the ruling. It applied its laws to a Cherokee named Corn Tassel for the murder of another Indian in Cherokee territory. This was a direct violation of the Supreme Court's decision.

The Supreme Court declared Georgia's action unconstitutional. Georgia ignored the Court again, and hanged Corn Tassel. U.S. President Andrew Jackson favored Georgia's action. He made no move to enforce the Supreme Court's rulings.

86

Suppose a similar situation arose today: A state government ignores a Supreme Court ruling and acts in a way the Court has said is unconstitutional. How do you think the state might be forced to act in accordance with the Supreme Court's decision? Should the U.S. president take action? The U.S. Congress? Write your answer and your reasoning in a paragraph.

© 2006 Walch Publishing

Factory Workers

During the first half of the 1800s, more and more Americans went to work in factories. Being a factory worker had its advantages and its disadvantages. In the columns below, list at least three of these advantages and at least three of these disadvantages.

Advantages   **Disadvantages**

87

© 2006 Walch Publishing

A Wave of Immigration

The bar graph below gives you some information about the U.S. population over a period of years. Study the bar graph. Then answer the questions that follow.

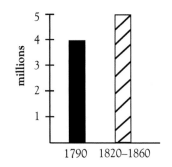

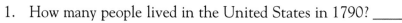

■ Total U.S population, 1790

▨ Total U.S. immigration, 1820–1860

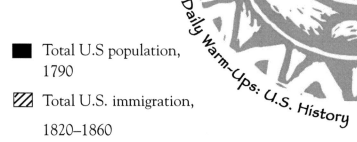

88

1. How many people lived in the United States in 1790? _____

2. How many people came to the United States as immigrants in the 40-year period from 1820 to 1860? _____

3. What accounts for this great wave of immigration? Write your answer in a paragraph.

© 2006 Walch Publishing

Sectional Conflict

The issue of slavery created increasing tensions between the North and the South. A series of compromises attempted but failed to lessen the tensions. For each outcome named below, give its date and its effect on the conflict over where slavery would be allowed.

1. Missouri Compromise _____

   _____

   _____

2. Compromise of 1850 _____

   _____

   _____

3. Kansas-Nebraska Act _____

   _____

   _____

89

© 2006 Walch Publishing

"Bleeding Kansas"

The Kansas-Nebraska Act was passed in 1854. People committed to opposing causes then poured into Kansas. Soon, Kansas became known as "Bleeding Kansas." Write one or two sentences as your answer to each question below.

1. What earlier compromise did the Kansas-Nebraska Act overturn? Name that compromise and describe its terms.

   _____

   _____

   _____

2. Why did the Kansas-Nebraska Act create the description "Bleeding Kansas"?

   _____

   _____

   _____

90

© 2006 Walch Publishing

The Election of 1860

The nation was deeply divided, North and South, in the 1860 presidential election. In fact, it was so divided that Democrats in the South and Democrats in the North named two different candidates for president. For each candidate and his party listed below, explain in a sentence his stand on slavery.

1. John C. Breckinridge, Democratic Party South _____

   _____

2. Stephen A. Douglas, Democratic Party North _____

   _____

3. Abraham Lincoln, Republican Party _____

   _____

4. John Bell, Constitutional Union Party _____

   _____

Daily Warm-Ups: U.S. History

91

© 2006 Walch Publishing

The Crittenden Compromise

In December 1860, U.S. Senator John Crittenden of Kentucky proposed a compromise that he hoped would avert a civil war between North and South.

- A new constitutional amendment would state that Congress had no power to interfere with slavery where it already existed and no power to abolish it from any state.

- The Missouri Compromise would be reinstated. Slavery would be banned from territorial lands north of 36°30' latitude and would be allowed in territorial lands south of 36°30' latitude.

92

The Crittenden Compromise failed. Why? Do you think the Compromise should have been adopted? Do you think that if it had been adopted, the Civil War would not have happened? As your answer, write a paragraph that explains your reasoning.

© 2006 Walch Publishing

Union and Secession

Abraham Lincoln was elected president of the United States in 1860. Jefferson Davis was elected president of the Confederate States of America in 1861. Each man expressed his thoughts on the Union and secession.

Abraham Lincoln: I hold that, in contemplation of universal law and of the Constitution, the Union of these states is perpetual. Perpetuity is implied, if not expressed, in the fundamental law of all national governments.

Jefferson Davis: Government rests upon the consent of the governed, and . . . it is the right of the people to alter or abolish governments whenever they become destructive of the ends for which they were established.

Which of these statements is based on principles expressed in the Declaration of Independence? Write your answer in a paragraph that explains your reasoning.

93

© 2006 Walch Publishing

Slavery Terms

The terms below relate to the conflict over slavery. Complete each sentence with a word from the box. You will not use all the words.

abolition	fugitive	popular sovereignty
free soil	nullification	secession

1. Under _____, voters in the territories could choose or reject slavery.

2. Slavery was not allowed in the _____ territories.

3. Northerners strongly objected to the _____ Slave Act of 1850.

4. The _____ movement wanted a complete end to slavery.

5. South Carolina put the _____ movement into motion when it left the Union in 1860.

94

© 2006 Walch Publishing

Slave and Free States

A number of new states joined the Union from the 1830s through the 1850s. On the lines after each state listed below, write the date it was admitted to the Union and also whether it was a free or a slave state.

1. Arkansas   _____   _____

2. California   _____   _____

3. Florida   _____   _____

4. Iowa   _____   _____

5. Michigan   _____   _____

6. Minnesota   _____   _____

7. Oregon   _____   _____

8. Texas   _____   _____

9. Wisconsin   _____   _____

95

What balance do you see among the new slave and free states? Do you see a trend in admissions? Write your answer in a few sentences.

© 2006 Walch Publishing

North v. South

When the Civil War began, the North had most of the advantages and some disadvantages. The South, too, enjoyed advantages and was burdened by disadvantages. For each statement below, write which side it applies to—North or South—and whether it was an advantage or a disadvantage to that side.

1. It had an agricultural economy.

   _____ _____

2. Its soldiers were mostly defending their own homeland.

   _____ _____

3. It had inept, indecisive commanders at first. _____ _____

4. It had many major rail lines. _____ _____

5. Its people were united and highly motivated.

   _____ _____

6. Public opinion at home was divided. _____ _____

7. It had a manufacturing economy. _____ _____

8. It had a small free population. _____ _____

96

© 2006 Walch Publishing

Civil and Revolutionary Wars

In the Revolutionary War, American colonists fought the British. The colonists fought to secure their way of life and their right to conduct their affairs as they saw fit. They fought on and for their new homeland. They kept on fighting for years, determined to wear down their opponents.

What similarities, if any, do you see between the colonists' fight against the British and the Confederates' fight against the North? Write your answer in a paragraph.

97

© 2006 Walch Publishing

Naming the War

In the North, the Civil War was often called the War of the Rebellion. In the South, the conflict was called the War of Northern Aggression. The names express the differences in how people in the North and in the South viewed the war. Explain in several sentences what view of the war each name expresses.

1. War of the Rebellion _____

_____

_____

2. War of Northern Aggression _____

_____

_____

_____

98

© 2006 Walch Publishing

Civil War Battles

Listed below are important Civil War battles. Next to each battle, write its date and tell which side—North or South—won.

1. First Bull Run _____ _____

2. Antietam _____ _____

3. Gettysburg _____ _____

4. Shiloh _____ _____

5. Petersburg _____ _____

6. Vicksburg _____ _____

7. Chancellorsville _____ _____

Bonus: Write one sentence for each battle that tells the battle's significance.

99

© 2006 Walch Publishing

Military Leaders

Both sides in the Civil War had some outstanding military leaders.
Match each commander's description to his name. Write the letter
of the correct name on the line provided.

a. Robert E. Lee
b. William T. Sherman
c. J. E. B. Stuart
d. Ulysses S. Grant
e. Thomas J. Jackson

____ 1. A realistic, tough cigar-chewer, he became head of the army in 1864.

____ 2. Dignified and well-dressed, he was a genius at strategy.

____ 3. Nicknamed Stonewall for his refusal to yield, his own men shot and killed
him by mistake.

____ 4. A believer in total war, he led his army on a path of destruction.

____ 5. A dashing, romantic cavalry leader, he was "the eyes and ears" of his
side's army.

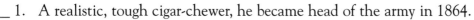

100

© 2006 Walch Publishing

The Emancipation Proclamation

Abraham Lincoln issued the Emancipation Proclamation in September 1862. The Proclamation declared that all slaves in areas "in rebellion against the United States" were free as of January 1, 1863. Lincoln issued the Proclamation to boost popular support for the war in the North and among the troops. The Proclamation did not actually free any slaves.

Write your answers to the following questions in a sentence for each.

1. Which slaves were not freed by the Emancipation Proclamation?

   _____

   _____

2. Why did Lincoln limit the effect of the Proclamation?

   _____

   _____

101

© 2006 Walch Publishing

Civil Liberties in Wartime

Civil liberties in the North suffered during the Civil War.
President Lincoln insisted on his right to prevent harm to the
Union by opponents of the war and/or supporters of the South.
Write a check mark next to each limit on civil rights that
occurred in the North during the war.

_____ 1. You are arrested and held without trial.

_____ 2. You are tried in a military court rather than a
civilian court.

_____ 3. You cannot vote, because elections have been canceled for the
duration of the war.

_____ 4. You are arrested for speaking in favor of making peace with the
Confederacy.

_____ 5. You are exiled to the Confederate states from your home state in
the North.

102

© 2006 Walch Publishing

Daily Warm-Ups: U.S. History

Grant's Victories

General Grant led his forces to a number of important victories for the North. Write the location next to each victory.

1. Fort Henry   _____

2. Fort Donelson _____

3. Vicksburg   _____

4. Port Hudson   _____

Why were these Northern victories especially devastating to the South? (Looking at these locations on a map will help you with your answer.) Write your answer in one or two sentences.

103

© 2006 Walch Publishing

Women of the Civil War

Women played significant roles in the Civil War—as spies, nurses, doctors, soldiers, and in other roles. Match each woman listed in the box with her description below. Write the letter of the correct name on the line.

a.	Belle Boyd	d.	Rose Greenhow
b.	Clara Barton	e.	Mary Walker
c.	Elizabeth Blackwell	f.	Sally Tompkins

_____ 1. first female American medical doctor, who set up what became the U.S. Sanitary Commission

_____ 2. society lady of Washington, D.C., who was a Southern spy

_____ 3. surgeon, spy for the Union, suffragette, and recipient of the Congressional Medal of Honor

_____ 4. the "Angel of the Battlefield" who began emergency care for wounded soldiers

_____ 5. teenage Confederate spy whom Stonewall Jackson made a captain

_____ 6. captain in the Confederate army who ran a hospital in Richmond

104

© 2006 Walch Publishing

Women and Reform

Women were very active in the abolition movement in the years leading up to, and during, the Civil War. They were active in the movement to extend civil rights to African Americans. Women's experiences spurred the women's rights movement.

Number these events from 1 through 7 in the order in which they occurred, with 1 being the earliest. Keep in mind the cause-and-effect factor to guide your answers.

_____ The Fifteenth Amendment is written and ratified.

_____ Women are not allowed to speak at reform meetings.

_____ Women in the abolition movement focus intently on women's suffrage.

_____ Women object to "adult male citizens" gaining the vote but not women.

_____ Women become early promoters of the abolition movement.

_____ Feminists are outraged when denial of voting rights to ex-slaves, but not to women, is banned.

_____ The Fourteenth Amendment is written and ratified.

105

© 2006 Walch Publishing

Phases of Reconstruction

Reconstruction in the South went through different phases from 1865 to 1877. The two phases below featured different policies, depending on which group was in control at the time. Describe in one or two sentences each of these Reconstruction policies.

1. Presidential Reconstruction

_____

_____

_____

_____

2. Radical Reconstruction

_____

_____

_____

_____

106

© 2006 Walch Publishing

Derogatory Nicknames

People in the Civil War and Reconstruction era invented some colorful names for people with various political views or activities. Match each description with the correct nickname from the box. Write the letter of the nickname on the line.

a. carpetbagger	c. doughface
b. copperhead	d. scalawag

____ 1. a Northerner who sided with the South during the Civil War, especially a congressman who supported slavery

____ 2. a Southern term for Southern whites who worked with Reconstruction governments

____ 3. a Northern opponent of the Civil War

____ 4. a Southern term for Northerners who went South to "help" with Reconstruction but were really there for their own benefit

© 2006 Walch Publishing

Reconstruction Chronology

Number the following Reconstruction events from 1 through 8 in the order in which they occurred, with 1 being the earliest.

_____ The Fourteenth Amendment is ratified.

_____ The final Civil Rights Act of this era is passed.

_____ The Freedmen's Bureau is established.

_____ The First Reconstruction Act is passed.

_____ The last federal troops withdraw from the South.

_____ The Ku Klux Klan forms.

_____ The first black member of the U.S. Congress is seated.

_____ The Thirteenth Amendment is ratified.

108

© 2006 Walch Publishing

African Americans of the Reconstruction

African Americans of the South were finally able to take prominent roles in society after the Civil War and emancipation. Match each description with the correct person. Write the letter of the person on the line.

a.	John H. Rock	d.	Charlotte Forten
b.	Joseph Rainey	e.	Robert Smalls
c.	P. B. S. Pinchback	f.	Blanche K. Bruce

____ 1. delivered a Confederate warship to Union forces during the war and later became a U.S. congressman

____ 2. became acting governor of Louisiana

____ 3. first black lawyer to argue a case before the U.S. Supreme Court

____ 4. a young person from Philadelphia who taught newly freed slaves of Port Royal, SC

____ 5. the second black U.S. Senator, from Mississippi

____ 6. the first black U.S. congressman

109

© 2006 Walch Publishing

A Sharecropper's Life

A new economic arrangement for farming developed in the South
after slavery ended. It was called sharecropping. For African
Americans, how did the conditions of being a sharecropper differ
from those of being a slave? Write **T** next to each statement below
about sharecroppers that is true. Write **F** next to each statement
that is false in any way.

____ 1. owned the land the family farmed

____ 2. went into debt to pay expenses

____ 3. worked when and in the way they chose

____ 4. were paid wages for their labor

____ 5. owned some, but not all, of the crops they grew

____ 6. were given food, clothing, and housing at no charge

110

© 2006 Walch Publishing

Black Codes

Southern states enacted a series of restrictive "black codes" in the 1860s after slavery ended. Write a check mark next to each statement below that correctly applies to these black codes.

_____ 1. You must have your employer's permission to leave the farm where you work.

_____ 2. You cannot marry legally.

_____ 3. You cannot testify in court.

_____ 4. You cannot attend a white people's church service.

_____ 5. You can be made to work for an employer against your will.

_____ 6. You cannot own any property.

111

© 2006 Walch Publishing

The "Stolen" Election

The initial results of the 1876 election for president were not conclusive. A second count of the electoral votes was made. Here are the results of both counts:

First vote
Samuel Tilden (Democrat): Popular vote, 4.3 million—Electoral vote, 184

Rutherford B. Hayes (Republican): Popular vote, 4 million—Electoral vote, 165

Second vote
Samuel Tilden (Democrat): Popular vote, 4.3 million—Electoral vote, 184

Rutherford B. Hayes (Republican): Popular vote, 4 million—Electoral vote, 185

112

Tilden won both the popular vote and the electoral vote, at first. But then Hayes took the electoral vote and became president. How did this happen? And what did this have to do with Reconstruction? Write your answer in a paragraph.

© 2006 Walch Publishing

Big Business

In the decades after the Civil War, big business grew rapidly and dominated the economy. Each term below relates to big business of this era. Write the letter of each term from the box next to its definition on the lines.

a. cartel	c. trust	e. holding company
b. monopoly	d. corporation	

_____ 1. control of a branch of business by one company

_____ 2. a form of business in which multiple stockholders own shares of the business

_____ 3. a combination of businesses that cooperate to limit competition and/or fix prices.

_____ 4. an arrangement in which many different companies are run by the same group of people

_____ 5. a corporation of corporations that hold shares in multiple companies

113

© 2006 Walch Publishing

Railroads and Public Lands

Railroads spread across the United States in the second half of the 1800s. Railroads made it possible to ship all kinds of goods all over the country fairly cheaply. This was a great benefit to the national economy, so the federal government promoted the building of rail lines.

In fact, the federal government gave huge tracts of public land to railroad companies in return for building rail lines across that land. After the railroad companies built their lines, they sold the land on either side of the tracks to settlers and others at a great profit.

114

The federal government reasoned that a nationwide rail system was a great national benefit. This justified giving public lands to private companies, the government said. Critics said that this was not right. They also said that railroad companies would build lines anyway, without being given public lands, because railroads were so profitable.

What do you think? Was the government justified in giving away these public lands? Write your answer in a paragraph that explains your reasoning.

© 2006 Walch Publishing

Business Tycoons

Big business of the late 1800s was dominated by "robber barons" and other wealthy tycoons. Match each industry below with the man who dominated it. Write the letter of the man on the line.

_____ 1. meatpacking

_____ 2. railroads

_____ 3. lumber

_____ 4. steel

_____ 5. oil

_____ 6. banking

a. Frederick Weyerhaeuser

b. John D. Rockefeller

c. Philip Armour

d. J. P. Morgan

e. William H. Vanderbilt

f. Andrew Carnegie

115

© 2006 Walch Publishing

Rating Rockefeller

John D. Rockefeller was a ruthless businessman. He declared to a Sunday school class:

> The growth of a large business is merely a survival of the fittest. . . . The American Beauty Rose can be produced in the splendor and fragrance which bring cheer to its beholder only by sacrificing the early buds which grow up around it. This is not an evil tendency in business.

To Rockefeller, the "American Beauty Rose" was his company, the Standard Oil Company. The "early buds" sacrificed to produce it were smaller competitors—businesses and individuals.

116

Rockefeller's business brought people a good product at a low price. And Rockefeller gave away half of his enormous fortune, funding worthy causes and establishing research institutes and a university.

How do you rate Rockefeller? Do the benefits of his consumer goods and his monetary donations outweigh the use and effects of his ruthless business practices? Write your answer in a paragraph that explains your reasoning.

© 2006 Walch Publishing

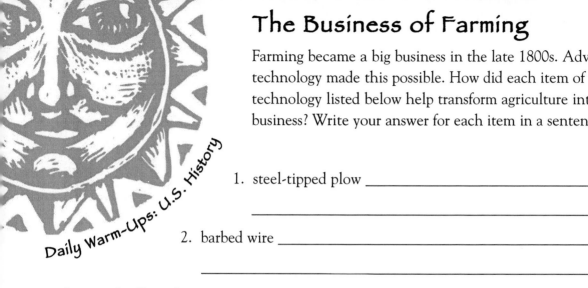

The Business of Farming

Farming became a big business in the late 1800s. Advances in farm technology made this possible. How did each item of farm technology listed below help transform agriculture into big business? Write your answer for each item in a sentence.

1. steel-tipped plow _____

_____

2. barbed wire _____

_____

3. windmills and pumps _____

_____

4. combine _____

_____

117

© 2006 Walch Publishing

Native American Leaders

Some notable Native American leaders of the post-Civil War decades are listed below. For each person, describe a significant role he played in Native American history.

1. Black Kettle _____

   _____

   _____

2. Chief Joseph _____

   _____

   _____

3. Red Cloud _____

   _____

   _____

4. Wovoka _____

   _____

   _____

118

© 2006 Walch Publishing

Native American Chronology

During the decades after the Civil War, the Great Plains Indians fought to keep their lands and their way of life. But the wave of non-Indian settlement was too much to stave off. Number each event below 1 through 9 in the order that it occurred in time, with 1 being the earliest.

_____ transcontinental railroad is completed

_____ Dawes Severalty Act is passed

_____ Battle of Little Big Horn is fought

_____ Wounded Knee massacre occurs

_____ Civil War ends

_____ Nez Perce flee toward Canada

_____ Homestead Act is passed

_____ Ghost Dance movement sweeps the Plains

_____ Black Hills gold rush starts

119

© 2006 Walch Publishing

City People

Look at the graph below.

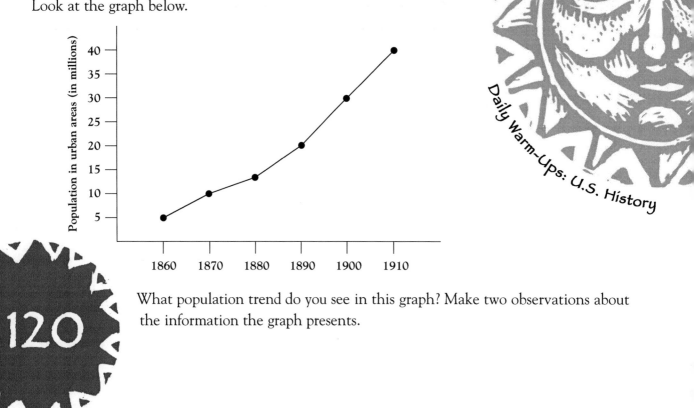

120

What population trend do you see in this graph? Make two observations about the information the graph presents.

© 2006 Walch Publishing

City Technology

Cities grew rapidly in the decades after the Civil War. Several innovations in technology helped make this growth possible. For each innovation listed below, write a sentence that describes its impact on city growth.

1. suspension bridge _____

   _____

2. steel-frame building _____

   _____

3. safety elevator _____

   _____

4. electric streetcar _____

   _____

121

© 2006 Walch Publishing

Immigration

The two pie charts below show the proportions of people who came to the United States from Europe in 1880 and in 1900.

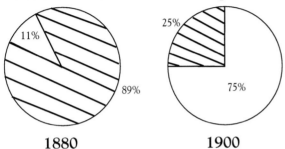

1880   1900

European Immigration from Region of Origin

122

Immigration from northern and western Europe (includes Great Britain, Ireland, Scandinavia, Germany)

Immigration from southern and eastern Europe (includes Poland, Russia, Italy, Baltic countries, others)

1. Who made up the largest group of immigrants from Europe in 1880?

   Who made up the largest group of immigrants from Europe in 1900?

2. What caused this change? What might have drawn these people to come to the United States? Write two or three sentences that explain your answer.

© 2006 Walch Publishing

Laborers and Unions

Various labor unions and organizations formed in the late 1800s and early 1900s. They pushed for workers' rights. Listed in the box below are three of these groups. Imagine you are each of the workers described below. For each, explain in one or two sentences which labor group you would join, and why.

> Knights of Labor
>
> American Federation of Labor (AFL)
>
> Industrial Workers of the World (IWW)

1. You are a skilled worker in a cigar-making factory.

2. You are an unskilled black worker in a garment factory.

3. You are a western miner, and you think there should be big unions for all workers. You also support the idea of a workers' revolution.

123

© 2006 Walch Publishing

A Rash of Strikes

The late 1800s saw numerous labor strikes. Workers in many different industries demanded better pay and working conditions. Match each strike in the box with its date and the industry involved. Write the letter of the industry on the line.

a. silver mines, 1892	d. agricultural machinery, 1884
b. railroad cars, 1894	e. coal mines, 1894
c. steel, 1892	f. railroads, 1877

_____ 1. Homestead strike

_____ 2. Great strike

_____ 3. Coeur d'Alene strike

_____ 4. Tracy City strike

_____ 5. Pullman strike

_____ 6. McCormick strike

124

© 2006 Walch Publishing

Notable Women

Several remarkable women captured national attention in the late 1800s. What do you know about the four women listed below? Write one or two sentences about each woman.

1. Victoria Woodhull _____

   _____

   _____

2. Belva Ann Lockwood _____

   _____

   _____

3. Mary Elizabeth Lease _____

   _____

   _____

4. Maria Harris Jones _____

   _____

   _____

125

© 2006 Walch Publishing

The Election of 1896

The 1896 campaign for U.S. president was dramatic. Voters in this election had many clear choices between the stands taken on the issues by the candidates and their parties.

Complete the chart below with the correct information about the 1896 presidential election.

126

	Bryan/Democrats	McKinley/Republicans
supported by whom?		
liberal or conservative?		
position on tariffs?		
region that supported him?		
urban or rural base?		
money backed by silver or gold?		

© 2006 Walch Publishing

Equal Rights in the South?

In 1877, Governor Wade Hampton of South Carolina declared:

> We will secure to every citizen, the lowest as well as
> the highest, black as well as white, full and equal
> protection in the enjoyment of all his rights under the
> Constitution.

Was this policy followed in the South in the years following Reconstruction? Write
your answer in a paragraph using specific examples.

127

© 2006 Walch Publishing

Modern Life

Listed below are new consumer products and conveniences. Write
a check mark next to each one that entered into many Americans'
lives in the late 1800s.

_____ 1. telephone

_____ 2. canned food

_____ 3. bicycle

_____ 4. television

_____ 5. department store

_____ 6. radio

_____ 7. electric light

_____ 8. movie theater

_____ 9. phonograph

_____ 10. pocket camera

_____ 11. electric refrigerator

_____ 12. automobile

128

© 2006 Walch Publishing

Overseas Expansion

In 1898, the United States expanded overseas. It acquired islands in the Caribbean Sea and the Pacific Ocean. Match each island or island group to its description. Write the letter of the description on the line.

_____ 1. Hawaii

_____ 2. Philippines

_____ 3. Cuba

_____ 4. Puerto Rico

a. island in the Caribbean where the U.S. army fought the Spanish military

b. island group in the Pacific whose last queen was overthrown in 1893

c. island group in the Caribbean that is a U.S. commonwealth today

d. island group in the Pacific where the United States fought a long and bitter guerrilla war

129

© 2006 Walch Publishing

Role-Players of the Spanish-American War

Each of the people named below played an important part in the Spanish-American War. Write one or two sentences for each that describes his role.

1. Jose Martí _____

   _____

2. Valeriano Weyler _____

   _____

3. William Randolph Hearst _____

   _____

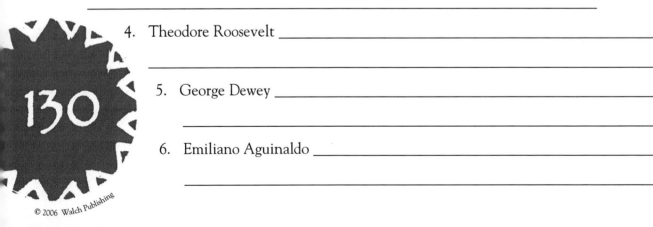

4. Theodore Roosevelt _____

   _____

5. George Dewey _____

   _____

6. Emiliano Aguinaldo _____

   _____

130

© 2006 Walch Publishing

Why Expand Overseas?

The U.S. expansion overseas was fueled by many factors: economic (**E**), military (**M**), foreign policy (**FP**), religious (**RE**), racist (**RA**), and the concept of manifest destiny (**MD**). Write the letter(s) of the motivating factor for each reason listed below.

_____ 1. American businesses needed overseas markets.

_____ 2. Missionaries wanted to spread Christianity.

_____ 3. Anglo-Saxon people were destined to rule over non-white people.

_____ 4. The United States needed to balance European activity overseas.

_____ 5. U.S. naval power needed to be modernized and expanded.

_____ 6. The United States was destined to keep on expanding.

131

© 2006 Walch Publishing

National Parks and the Frontier

These two important things happened in the United States in 1890:

- The U.S. Census Bureau announced that the frontier no longer existed. The United States had no more great stretches of unsettled land.

- Yosemite and Sequoia became the second and third U.S. national parks. (Yellowstone had been first, in 1872.)

In what ways are these two events related? How does the opening of national parks relate to the closing of the frontier? Write a paragraph as your answer.

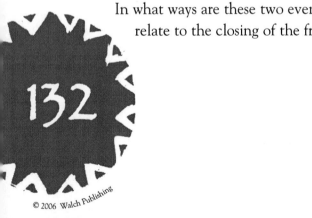

© 2006 Walch Publishing

Foreign Policy Policies

The United States became very involved in Latin America in the early 1900s. Three different U.S. presidents followed three variations of policy in this region. Describe each of these policies in one or two sentences.

1. the Big Stick—Theodore Roosevelt _____
   _____
   _____

2. Dollar Diplomacy—William H. Taft _____
   _____
   _____

3. Missionary, or Moral, Diplomacy—Woodrow Wilson _____
   _____
   _____

133

© 2006 Walch Publishing

Interventions in Latin America

Listed below are some of the Latin American nations where U.S. troops moved in during the early 1900s. Match each nation to the correct event. Write the letter of the event on the line.

_____ 1. Cuba

_____ 2. Nicaragua

_____ 3. Panama

_____ 4. Haiti

134

a. U.S. warships allowed a revolution to take place here in 1903.

b. U.S. troops occupied this island nation from 1915 to 1934.

c. After winning a war on this island nation in 1898, U.S. troops stayed on and off until 1922.

d. The United States took over customs, and U.S. troops occupied this Central American nation from 1910 to 1933.

© 2006 Walch Publishing

The Progressive Amendments

Four amendments were added to the U.S. Constitution during the Progressive Era. They are listed below with their dates of ratification. Write a description of each one.

1. Sixteenth Amendment (1913)

   _____

   _____

2. Seventeenth Amendment (1913)

   _____

   _____

3. Eighteenth Amendment (1919)

   _____

   _____

4. Nineteenth Amendment (1920)

   _____

   _____

135

© 2006 Walch Publishing

The Muckrakers

Reform-minded journalists of the Progressive Era were often called muckrakers. They investigated and then exposed problems in many areas of U.S. society. Write the letter of each reforming writer next to the subject she or he famously exposed.

_____ 1. local political corruption

_____ 2. the meatpacking industry

_____ 3. mental hospitals

_____ 4. beef and tobacco trusts

_____ 5. Standard Oil Company

_____ 6. life in the slums

_____ 7. railroads versus farmers

a. Jacob Riis

b. Charles Edward Russell

c. Lincoln Steffens

d. Ida Tarbell

e. Frank Norris

f. Upton Sinclair

g. Nellie Bly

136

© 2006 Walch Publishing

Free Speech—or Not

Eugene V. Debs ran for U.S. president five times as the Socialist Party candidate. He ran in 1904, 1908, 1912, 1916, and 1920. He got the most votes in 1920—nearly 1 million—even though he was in jail at the time! He was serving a sentence of 10 years, although he was released after 20 months.

Write your answers to the following questions in one or two sentences.

1. Why was Debs in jail?

   _____

   _____

   _____

2. Do you think Debs was convicted and jailed justifiably?

   _____

   _____

   _____

137

© 2006 Walch Publishing

Being Vice President

Theodore Roosevelt was elected U.S. vice president in 1900. He became president when President McKinley was assassinated in 1901. John Nance Garner was elected U.S. vice president in 1932. Here's what they had to say about the office of vice president.

Theodore Roosevelt: "The Vice Presidency is a most honorable office, but for a young man there is not much to do."

John Nance Garner: "The vice presidency isn't worth a pitcher of warm spit."

1. Describe the duties and role of the U.S. vice president.

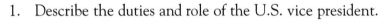

2. Do you think the duties and role of the vice president are different today from what they were in Roosevelt's and Garner's times?

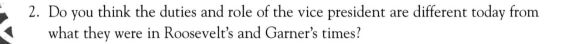

138

© 2006 Walch Publishing

The United States and World War I

At first, the United States wanted to stay neutral in World War I. But as events unfolded, the United States was ultimately drawn in. Number each event below from 1 through 8 in the order in which they occurred, with 1 being the earliest.

_____ A U-boat sinks the British passenger liner *Lusitania*.

_____ The Zimmerman telegram becomes public.

_____ Woodrow Wilson is reelected on the slogan "He Kept Us Out of War."

_____ Great Britain imposes a naval blockade on German shipping.

_____ Germany resumes unrestricted submarine warfare.

_____ The United States enters the war.

_____ German submarines start attacking ships without warning.

_____ Germany promises to stop unrestricted submarine warfare.

139

© 2006 Walch Publishing

Technology of the Great War

New war technologies were used for the first time in World War I. They made this "Great War" horribly destructive. Write a check mark next to each item of war technology that was first used in this war.

_____ tank

_____ U-boat

_____ aircraft carrier

_____ warplane

_____ radar

_____ atomic bomb

_____ long-range artillery

_____ poison gas

_____ machine gun

_____ bazooka

140

© 2006 Walch Publishing

Making Peace, Preventing War

After World War I ended, U.S. President Woodrow Wilson was very concerned about the peace agreement that would be made. Here are several things he said:

"What the Germans used [in this war] were toys as compared with what would be used in the next war."

"I can predict with absolute certainty that within another generation there will be another world war" if the U.S. Senate did not approve the League of Nations by approving the Versailles peace treaty.

Were these accurate predictions? Write your answer in a paragraph that explains your reasoning.

141

© 2006 Walch Publishing

Twenties Talk

Below is a list of common words from the 1920s. Write each word from the box on the line after its definition.

bootlegger	flapper	Tin Lizzie
speakeasy	flaming youth	

1. a Model T Ford: _____

2. a place where alcoholic drinks were sold, illegally, during Prohibition: _____

3. a young "new woman" of the 1920s who wore short hair and short hems:
   _____

4. a person who made, sold, and/or transported for sale alcoholic drinks, illegally, during Prohibition: _____

5. the unconventional, partying, and drinking young people of the 1920s:
   _____

142

The Full Pail and the Full Garage

Herbert Hoover was elected U.S. president in 1928. During the campaign, he declared:

> "The slogan of progress has changed from the full dinner pail to the full garage."

What does this mean? What was "the full dinner pail"? What is the significance of "the full garage"? Write your answer in a paragraph.

143

© 2006 Walch Publishing

Problematic Predictions

Herbert Hoover was not very good at making predictions. In 1924, as U.S. secretary of commerce, he said the following about radio broadcasting:

> "I believe the quickest way to kill radio broadcasting would be to use it for direct advertising. The reader of a newspaper has an option whether he will read an ad or not, but if a speech by the president is to be used as the meat in a sandwich of two patent-medicine advertisements, there will be no radio left."

In 1928, as U.S. president, he said this about the U.S. economy:

> "Given a chance to go forward with the policies of the last eight years, we shall soon, with the help of God, be in sight of the day when poverty will be banished from this nation."

144

What was very inaccurate about these Hoover statements? Write one or two sentences for each statement as your answer.

© 2006 Walch Publishing

The Great Migration

Look at the chart below. It shows the black populations of Detroit, Michigan, and Chicago, Illinois, in 1910 and 1930.

	1910	1930
Detroit	6,000	120,000
Chicago	44,000	235,000

1. What is the percentage increase in the black population in Detroit between 1910 and 1930? _____

   What is that percentage increase in Chicago?

   _____

2. This same pattern was repeated in many other cities. What caused this "Great Migration" of African Americans? What "push" factors made them feel they needed to leave the South? What "pull" factors made them want to go North?

145

© 2006 Walch Publishing

The Harlem Renaissance

The period of great creativity in African-American arts during the 1920s is called the Harlem Renaissance. Outstanding figures of that renaissance are listed below. Next to each name, write the branch of art he or she is best known for: **music, poetry, painting,** or **novels.**

1. Langston Hughes   _____

2. Zora Neale Hurston   _____

3. Jacob Lawrence   _____

4. Duke Ellington   _____

5. Romare Bearden   _____

6. Bessie Smith   _____

7. Jean Toomer   _____

8. Countee Cullen   _____

146

© 2006 Walch Publishing

The Scopes Trial

The famous Scopes trial took place in 1925. John Scopes, a high school teacher, was charged with breaking a Tennessee law that said the following:

> [It is] unlawful for any teacher . . . to teach any theory that denies the story of the divine creation of man as taught in the Bible, and to teach instead that man has descended from a lower order of animals.

Do you think this law violates the First Amendment of the U.S. Constitution? Reread that amendment, then write your answer in a paragraph that explains your reasoning.

147

© 2006 Walch Publishing

Who Was I?

Write the name of each woman from the box on the line next to her description.

Isadora Duncan	Jeannette Rankin
Alice Paul	Margaret Sanger

1. I tirelessly promoted birth control, especially to help poor women limit the size of their families. Who was I?

   _____

2. I pressed for the addition of an Equal Rights Amendment to the U.S. Constitution. Who was I? _____

3. A free spirit, I had two children without getting married, while creating the art form now called modern dance. Who was I? _____

4. I was the first woman elected to the U.S. Congress, in 1917, and I voted against entering World War I. Who was I? _____

148

© 2006 Walch Publishing

Presidential Nicknames

Men who ran for U.S. president in the 1920s acquired some apt nicknames. For each man listed below, explain in one or two sentences why he earned his nickname.

1. Calvin Coolidge—Silent Cal _____

_____

_____

2. Al Smith—the Happy Warrior _____

_____

_____

3. Herbert Hoover—the Great Engineer _____

_____

_____

149

© 2006 Walch Publishing

Nativism

The following events took place in the United States during the 1920s:

- Membership in the Ku Klux Klan rose from 100,000 in 1920 to almost 5 million in 1924.

- Nicola Sacco and Bartolomeo Vanzetti were found guilty of murder and executed.

- The Johnson Act/Emergency Quota Act of 1921 and the National Origins Act of 1924 passed. They set quotas on immigration by national origin.

150

All of these events were related to an unpleasant movement that became widespread in the 1920s—**nativism.** What is nativism? How are the events above related to nativism? Write your answer to these questions in a paragraph.

© 2006 Walch Publishing

Daily Warm-Ups: U.S. History

The Great Depression Arrives

The events described below all relate to the Great Depression. Number the events from 1 though 6 in the order in which they occurred, with 1 being the earliest.

____ Franklin D. Roosevelt is elected U.S. president.

____ The stock market crashes—stock prices plummet.

____ The Second Hundred Days is launched.

____ Government help goes to banks and businesses, not to individual people.

____ Millions of Americans invest in the stock market, many on margin.

____ The New Deal begins.

151

© 2006 Walch Publishing

The New Deal

Read each statement below about the New Deal. Write **T** next to each statement that is true. Write **F** next to each that is false in any way.

_____ 1. increased federal workers' salaries

_____ 2. brought electricity to rural America

_____ 3. paid young men to plant trees

_____ 4. limited union membership

_____ 5. set up an old-age pension system

_____ 6. put closed factories under government management

_____ 7. regulated the stock market

_____ 8. insured people's bank accounts

152

© 2006 Walch Publishing

The New Deal Today

Each agency and act below began as a New Deal program and still exists today. Circle the letter of the term that correctly completes each statement.

1. The Securities and Exchange Commission (SEC) regulates

    a. farming. b. the stock market. c. labor unions.

2. The Federal Deposit Insurance Corporation (FDIC) deals with

    a. money in banks. b. old-age pensions. c. wage levels.

3. The Tennessee Valley Authority (TVA) operates

    a. factories. b. national parks. c. dams.

4. The Social Security Act deals with

    a. old-age pensions. b. job security. c. education.

153

© 2006 Walch Publishing

Stock Market Terms

The stock market crash of 1929 triggered the Great Depression.
The terms in the box below are all about stocks and the market.
Complete each sentence with the correct word from the box.
Write the word on the line.

margin	panic	depression	stock market

1. A _____ is the business of buying and selling shares in corporations.

2. During a _____, business is slow and people lose their jobs.

3. When people buy stock on _____, they pay only part of the price at the time they buy.

4. A _____ is a sudden widespread fright about money matters.

154

© 2006 Walch Publishing

Events and Economics

Look at the chart below. (Gross national product, GNP, is the total value of all goods and services produced in the nation during a period of time—in this chart, one year.) Then answer the questions in one or two sentences.

U.S. Economy, 1929–1944

	GNP	Unemployment rate
1929	$103.7 billion	3.6%
1940	$99.7 billion	14.6%
1942	$159 billion	9.9%
1944	$211.4 billion	1.2%

1. What accounts for the economic changes between 1929 and 1940?

2. What accounts for the economic changes between 1940 and 1942?

3. What accounts for the economic changes between 1942 and 1944?

155

© 2006 Walch Publishing

Moving Toward War

Each pair of sentences below relates to the United States being drawn toward and into World War II. One sentence describes a cause. The other describes an effect. Label the cause (**C**) and the effect (**E**) for each pair of sentences.

_____ 1A. U.S. navy ships protect ships carrying U.S. military supplies to Europe.

_____ 1B. The United States sells military supplies to the European Allies.

_____ 2A. Japan signs alliances with Germany and Italy, and invades French Indochina.

_____ 2B. The United States places embargoes on trade with Japan.

_____ 3A. U.S. public opinion turns in favor of entering World War II.

_____ 3B. Japan attacks Pearl Harbor.

_____ 4A. Germany declares war on the United States.

_____ 4B. U.S. troops land in Europe.

156

© 2006 Walch Publishing

The Tide Turns

The tide of war started to turn in favor of the Allies in 1943. Number each event below from 1 through 7 in the order in which they occurred, with 1 being the earliest.

____ Soviet troops start driving the invading German army back toward the nations of Eastern Europe.

____ The Allies conduct an intense bombing campaign against the city of Dresden in Germany.

____ The Soviets move into Germany on the east.

____ The Allies invade Italy.

____ Germany surrenders.

____ Allied forces drive the Germans out of North Africa.

____ The Allies invade France on D-Day.

157

© 2006 Walch Publishing

War Words

Some new words became part of the English language during World War II. Write a definition of each word listed below that explains its meaning and also its World War II origin.

1. blitzkrieg _____

_____

2. ersatz _____

_____

3. gobbledygook _____

_____

4. radar _____

_____

5. snafu _____

_____

158

© 2006 Walch Publishing

Cold War Hot Spots

Cold War conflicts cropped up around the world. Circle the place where each of these problems occurred.

1. The United States engineered a coup to oust a nationalist and reinstall the pro-Western shah here in 1953.

   a. Iraq b. Egypt c. Iran

2. The United States sent aid in 1949 to help this democratic nation fight a guerrilla war against communists.

   a. Greece b. India c. Nicaragua

3. U.S. forces led a United Nations coalition army here to push back an invasion by a communist government from the north.

   a. Vietnam b. Korea c. Somalia

4. A crisis over missiles here in 1962 nearly caused nuclear war between the United States and the Soviet Union.

   a. Turkey b. Cuba c. China

159

© 2006 Walch Publishing

War Comes to Vietnam

U.S. involvement in Vietnam started small. It then grew to great proportions. Trace this growth by writing several sentences that tell how each U.S. president named below involved the United States in Vietnam.

1. President Truman _____
   _____

2. President Eisenhower _____
   _____

3. President Kennedy _____
   _____

4. President Johnson _____
   _____

5. President Nixon _____
   _____

160

© 2006 Walch Publishing

The Gulf of Tonkin

The real escalation in Vietnam took place after President Johnson said that North Vietnamese gunboats had attacked U.S. destroyers in Vietnam's Gulf of Tonkin. This attack was unprovoked, Johnson said. In response, the U.S. Congress passed the Tonkin Gulf Resolution:

> Resolved . . . that the Congress approves and supports the determination of the President, as Commander in Chief, to take all necessary measures to repel any armed attack against the forces of the United States and to prevent further aggression.

1. In your opinion, did this resolution authorize the steps President Johnson and President Nixon took in escalating the war in Vietnam?

2. We now know that North Vietnamese gunboats most likely did not attack U.S. warships in the Gulf of Tonkin. U.S. forces had initiated hostilities in that area. How does this affect your opinion in question 1 above?

161

© 2006 Walch Publishing

The Great Society

President Lyndon Johnson launched his Great Society program to help Americans who were disadvantaged. Write the letter of each description next to the matching Great Society program.

a. provided medical care for older people
b. helped poor people pay for health care
c. provided preschool for poor children
d. trained unemployed teenagers for jobs
e. barred discrimination in public places
f. helped African Americans secure their right to vote

____ 1. Civil Rights Act

____ 2. Operation Headstart

____ 3. Medicare

____ 4. Youth Corps

____ 5. Voting Rights Act

____ 6. Medicaid

162

© 2006 Walch Publishing

Civil Rights Terms

The civil rights movement of the 1960s used several types of tactics. Write a definition of each of the tactics named below. Then give an example of its use during the civil rights era.

1. sit-in _____

   _____

2. boycott _____

   _____

3. freedom ride _____

   _____

4. passive resistance _____

   _____

Another approach was the concept of **black power.** Explain this in one or two sentences.

_____

_____

163

© 2006 Walch Publishing

Women and the Civil Rights Movement

Young people with heartfelt ideals were a big part of the civil rights movement in the 1960s. They were also a big part of the larger protest movement about many aspects of society that grew from the initial civil rights movement. Young women active in this protest movement began to notice something about their role in these activities. Soon, a new women's rights movement emerged.

1. What about women's roles in the civil rights movement inspired the new women's rights movement?

   _____

   _____

   _____

164

2. What parallel do you see among these women and the women who were active in the abolition and voting rights movements in the 1860s and 1870s?

   _____

   _____

   _____

© 2006 Walch Publishing

Plessy and Brown

In 1896, the U.S. Supreme Court ruled that the U.S. Constitution allowed segregated schools. The Court said in the case *Plessy* v. *Ferguson*:

> If the civil and political rights of both races be equal, one cannot be inferior to the other civilly or politically. If one race be inferior to the other socially, the Constitution of the United States cannot put them upon the same plane.

In 1954, the Supreme Court ruled that segregation of schools violated the U.S. Constitution. The Court said in the case *Brown* v. *Board of Education of Topeka*:

> We conclude that in the field of public education the doctrine of "separate but equal" has no place. Separate educational facilities are inherently unequal.

How is the Court's reasoning in these two cases different? What do you think might account for these differences?

165

© 2006 Walch Publishing

The Space Age

The United States and the U.S.S.R. raced against each other to explore space in the late 1950s and the 1960s. Match each space vehicle named below with the details about it.

_____ 1. *Telstar 1*

_____ 2. *Freedom 7*

_____ 3. *Apollo 11*

_____ 4. *Vostok 11*

_____ 5. *Sputnik*

_____ 6. *Tiros 1*

_____ 7. *Lunik 2*

a. 1957, U.S.S.R., first artificial satellite launch

b. 1959, U.S.S.R., first earth object to land on the moon

c. 1960, U.S., first weather satellite

d. 1961, U.S.S.R., first human being in space

e. 1961, U.S., first U.S. astronaut in space

f. 1962, U.S., first commercial communications satellite

g. 1969, U.S., first human beings on the moon

166

© 2006 Walch Publishing

The Warren Court

The U.S. Supreme Court under Chief Justice Earl Warren issued a series of decisions with far-reaching effects. Match each case with the right it confirmed. Write the correct letter of the decision on the line next to its case.

_____ 1. *Roe* v. *Wade*

_____ 2. *Gideon* v. *Wainwright*

_____ 3. *Miranda* v. *Arizona*

_____ 4. *Baker* v. *Carr*

_____ 5. *Griswold* v. *Connecticut*

a. right to have a lawyer present when being questioned by police

b. individual's right to privacy

c. free legal counsel for poor people accused of a crime

d. "one man, one vote" for voting districts

e. women's right to abortion

167

© 2006 Walch Publishing

U.S. Foreign Policy

Match each U.S. president to the foreign policy elements associated with his term in office. Write the letter of the correct policy elements on the line.

____ 1. Richard Nixon

____ 2. Jimmy Carter

____ 3. Ronald Reagan

____ 4. George H. W. Bush

168

a. oil crisis, Camp David, Panama Canal, Iran hostages

b. Gulf War, Somalia, Yugoslavia

c. China visit, détente, SALT I

d. "evil empire," Iran-Contra, "Star Wars"

© 2006 Walch Publishing

"Red Scares"

Two "red scares" swept the nation in the 1920s and the 1950s. People across the nation became highly fearful of communists within the United States. These "red scares" were promoted by U.S. Attorney General A. Mitchell Palmer in the 1920s and U.S. Senator Joseph McCarthy in the 1950s.

In the 1920s, Palmer targeted anyone with anarchist (protesting the government) ideas, as well as radicals or people with leftist ideas from foreign countries. During this time, Palmer instituted "Palmer raids," in which Justice Department agents and local police burst into meeting places and people's homes (mostly by warrant), searched and seized books and papers, and took people into custody; local police often did these things on their own without warrants. About 6,000 people were arrested; of those, only 556 were deported.

In the 1950s, McCarthy targeted anyone with left-leaning ideas. His group made unsupported accusations. Many lives and careers were ruined. For example, nearly 500 State Department employees were fired with no proof of wrongdoing. Many Hollywood figures were blacklisted and could not work.

Why do you think the American people supported such attacks on civil liberties and the use of smear tactics? Do you think this type of movement could sweep the nation again? If so, under what circumstances?

169

© 2006 Walch Publishing

A Memorable Year

The year 1968 stands out in U.S. history. Significant and shocking events occurred one after another. Describe these events of 1968 in the following areas in one or several sentences for each.

1. Vietnam War key event _____

   _____

   _____

2. presidential politics _____

   _____

   _____

3. assassinations _____

   _____

   _____

4. violence _____

   _____

   _____

170

© 2006 Walch Publishing

The Young Generations

Young people in the 1920s and the 1960s broke away from social conventions and shocked many older people. Compare these two young generations by completing the chart below.

	Hair and clothing	Dance	Attitude	Drug use
Young people of the 1920s				
Young people of the 1960s				

171

© 2006 Walch Publishing

Protecting the Environment

Under President Nixon, the U.S. Congress passed many far-reaching laws to protect the environment. Write a description of each congressional action on the environment listed below.

1. Clean Air Act amendments, 1970

   _____

   _____

2. Environmental Protection Agency, 1970

   _____

   _____

3. Endangered Species Act, 1973

   _____

   _____

4. Water Quality Improvement Act, 1970

   _____

   _____

172

© 2006 Walch Publishing

Seventies and Eighties

The decades of the 1970s and the 1980s both earned their own distinctive nicknames. Explain each of these nicknames in one or two sentences. Then answer the question that follows.

1. 1970s—the Me Decade

   _____

   _____

2. 1980s—the Greed Decade

   _____

   _____

What nickname would you give to the decade of the 1990s? Write your answer in one or two sentences that explain your reasoning.

_____

_____

173

© 2006 Walch Publishing

Impeachment

In the twentieth century, two U.S. presidents were impeached or nearly impeached. Explore that process by writing descriptions and then answering the question below.

1. Describe the process of impeachment as set up by the U.S. Constitution.

   _____

   _____

2. Describe the near-impeachment of President Nixon.

   _____

   _____

3. Describe the actual impeachment of President Clinton.

   _____

   _____

4. In your opinion, should either Nixon or Clinton have been found guilty of the charges against him?

174

Daily Warm-Ups: U.S. History

© 2006 Walch Publishing

The "New Immigration"

Look at the bar graph below.

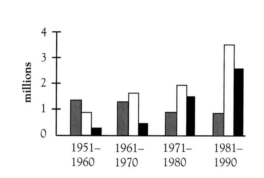

- Europe
- Americas
- Asia

Immigration to the United States, by Region

What changing patterns do you see in immigration from Asia, the Americas, and Europe from 1950 to 1990? Make at least two observations about this. What factors caused these changes?

© 2006 Walch Publishing

Third-Party Candidates

Third-party candidates can have big impacts on presidential elections. Look at the three pie charts below.

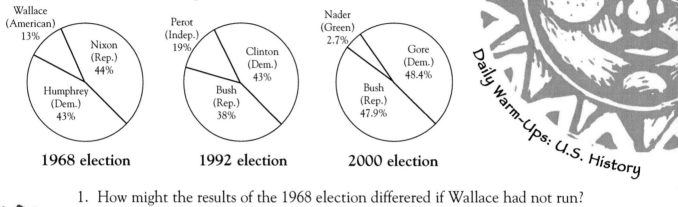

1. How might the results of the 1968 election differered if Wallace had not run?

2. How might the results of the 1992 election differered if Perot had not run?

3. How might the results of the 2000 election differered if Nader had not run?

176

© 2006 Walch Publishing

Presidents, Presidents, Presidents

Do you have trouble remembering which U.S. presidents served before and after other U.S. presidents? One way to remember is to make up a catchy or nonsense sentence. Each word in the sentence starts with the first letter of a president's last name. The words in the sentence are in chronological order of the presidents' terms in office. The earliest president in the sequence comes first.

Consider, for example, the presidents from the 1950s through the early 2000s: Eisenhower, Kennedy, Johnson, Nixon, Carter Reagan, Bush, Clinton, Bush

Here are some sample nonsense sentences:

Every **k**angaroo **j**umps **n**ightly: Eisenhower, Kennedy, Johnson, Nixon

No **c**at **r**eads **b**ogus **c**omic **b**ooks: Nixon, Carter, Reagan, Bush, Clinton, Bush

Jail **n**o **c**hild **r**eporters **b**efore **C**hristmas: Johnson, Nixon, Carter, Reagan, Bush, Clinton

Create your own presidential sentences. (They can be for sequences of presidents in other years, not just the presidents listed here.) Share your creations with classmates. Can they identify the presidents in your sentence?

177

© 2006 Walch Publishing

2000: The Controversial Election

The 2000 presidential election was the closest in U.S. history. The results were highly controversial. Number the events below from 1 through 7 in the order they occurred, with 1 being the earliest.

_____ The Bush campaign sued in court to stop the recount.

_____ The U.S. Supreme Court ordered the recounts to end.

_____ Al Gore won the popular vote.

_____ An automatic recount of the Florida popular vote began.

_____ George W. Bush became president-elect.

_____ Initial results gave the popular vote victory in Florida to George W. Bush.

_____ The Florida Supreme Court ordered the recounts to continue.

178

© 2006 Walch Publishing

The War on Terror

Days after the horrific attacks of September 11, 2001, the U.S. Congress passed the "Use of Force" Resolution. Its key provision reads:

> [T]he President is authorized to use all necessary and appropriate force against those nations, organizations, or persons he determines planned, authorized, committed, or aided the terrorist attacks that occurred on September 11, 2001, or harbored such organizations or persons, in order to prevent any future acts of international terrorism against the United States by such nations, organizations or persons.

The Bush administration has used this resolution to justify a wide range of actions undertaken as part of the war on terror. One example of such action is eavesdropping on U.S. citizens' communications with people overseas, without court approval. What do you think? Does the U.S. president have power to take whatever actions he deems necessary to conduct the war on terror? Or are his actions limited under law or under the Constitution? Write your answer in a paragraph that explains your reasoning.

179

© 2006 Walch Publishing

Thinking About History

Write a paragraph that explains your opinion about one of these quotations about the study of history. For the Twain and Ulrich quotations, offer at least one example from history in support of your opinion. For the McCullough quotation, give examples of history (fact or historical novel) you have enjoyed reading and history you have not enjoyed reading.

To arrive at a just estimate of a renowned man's character, one must judge it by the standards of his time, not ours.

— Mark Twain

Well-behaved women rarely make history.

— Laurel Thatcher Ulrich

No harm's done to history by making it something someone would want to read.

— David McCullough

180

© 2006 Walch Publishing

1. 1. frigid, harsh; 2. marine: cool, wet, mild;
    3. semidesert; 4. weather extremes, moderate
    rainfall; 5. mild, humid; 6. good rainfall, cold
    winters, warm summers

2. 1. T 2. T 3. F; They domesticated dogs and llamas.
    4. F; The ice did not reach to Central America.
    5. F; Remains show that the earliest peoples
    included meat in their diet. 6. T

3. Answers will vary. Major examples: Mountains:
    Rockies, Appalachians, Coastal Ranges, Sierra
    Nevada, Cascades; Rivers: Mississippi, Missouri,
    Ohio, St. Lawrence, Arkansas, Rio Grande,
    Colorado, Columbia; Lakes: Great Lakes, Lake
    Champlain, Great Salt Lake; Bays/Gulfs: Gulf of
    Mexico, Hudson Bay, Chesapeake Bay; Plains:
    Central, Great

4. 1. Mesa Verde 2. Cahokia 3. Tikal 4. Great Lakes
    5. Tenochtitlán 6. Cuzco

5. 1. M, A 2. M, A, I 3. A, I 4. M, A 5. M, A, I
    6. M, A, I 7. M, A 8. M, A, I 9. M, A

10. M, A, I

6. Events should be numbered in this order: 6, 2, 4,
    8, 1, 5, 3, 7

7. 1. e 2. i 3. f 4. a 5. h 6. d 7. b 8. c 9. g

8. 1. an elaborate ceremonial feast with lavish gift-
    giving 2. a large village of stone-and-clay buildings
    3. a North American Indian chief, especially of
    the Algonquian tribes 4. corn, a staple crop
    5. a hard volcanic rock used to make razor-sharp
    weapons and tools a prized trade item 6. a
    "floating garden" of the Aztecs on marshy lake
    edges 7. a set of knotted strings used by Incas to
    keep records

9. The following should be checked: 1, 3, 4, 6, 7, 9

10. 1. b 2. d 3. a 4. e 5. c

11. Choice of peoples will vary. Eastern Woodlands
    include Algonquin, Abenaki, and Huron. Plains
    include Cheyenne, Pawnee, Crow, Blackfoot,
    Sioux, and Nez Perce. Northwest Coast includes
    Chinook, Haida, Kwakiutl, and Tlingit.

Arctic/Subarctic includes Aleut, Cree, and Inuit. Southwest includes Hopi, Navajo, Mohave, and Pueblo. Southeast includes Cherokee, Choctaw, Creek, and Seminole.

12. Personal accounts will vary. Students can draw on additional material from their textbooks. This should be just a quick snapshot of a day.

13. 1. b 2. a 3. b 4. c 5. a

14. 1. Europe 2. Americas 3. Europe 4. Americas 5. Americas 6. Africa 7. Europe 8. Africa 9. Africa 10. Americas 11. Europe 12. Africa 13. Americas 14. Europe 15. Americas 16. Africa

15. All factors are advantages for the Spanish and disadvantages for the Aztecs and Incas. Sentences will vary. 1. The Spanish had overwhelming superiority—guns and cannon, horses, armor, all of which were unknown to the Aztecs and Incas. 2. The Aztecs believed that Cortés was the god Quetzalcoatl who was foretold to return from the east from across the sea. Cortés arrived on the exact day predicted by Aztec prophets. 3. Cortés was able to secure the help of various native groups who resented Aztec imperial rule. The Incas were embroiled in a succession struggle and so did not meet the Spanish with a united front. 4. Cortés agreed to take just a share of Aztec wealth at first, but then reneged on that agreement. Pizarro promised to release the Inca emperor on payment of a fabulous ransom, but he had the emperor killed after receiving the treasure. 5. The Aztecs and Incas had no immunity to the European diseases that the Spanish brought with them; by the time of the final battles with the Spanish, the Aztec population had been decimated by disease.

16. Caboto (Italy)—England; 1497; Canada (Newfoundland, Nova Scotia). Columbo (Italy)—Spain; 1492; Caribbean Islands. Cabral—Portugal; 1500; Brazil. Champlain—France; 1609; Canada (St. Lawrence River). Hudson (England)—

Netherlands; 1609; Hudson River, Nova Scotia.

17. 1. Merchants wanted a more efficient sea route to the highly profitable spices of the Far East, and governments supported this as a way of increasing national wealth. 2. As central governments gained strength, national pride grew; nations desired colonies to increase their power and wealth; rival nations didn't want their competition to gain on them in power and wealth. 3. Many Europeans were strongly motivated to spread Christianity wherever possible. 4. The design of ships (for example, the caravel) and navigational tools (such as the magnetic compass, the astrolabe, and the quadrant) greatly improved during this time, making ambitious cross-ocean voyages feasible.

18. 1. Columbus is in the Caribbean; Japan is on the other side of the planet. Of course, Cuba and Japan are not the same. 2. The Caribbean Islands did not have much gold or gems and were not the source of the East Indies spices that Columbus hoped to find. 3. This statement is true about the Arawak/ Taino peoples, but quite wrong about the fierce, warlike Caribs nearby.

19. St. Augustine—1565; Spain. Jamestown—1607; England. Quebec—1608; France. Santa Fe—1610; Spain. Plymouth—1620; England. New Amsterdam—1626; Netherlands. Spain is active in the South and Southwest; England's activity is focused on the eastern seaboard; France is active in Canada; the Dutch are focused on New York. Sentences will vary.

20. 1. about 17,000 2. Europeans had been fishing off the coast of New England all during the 1500s and early 1600s. They sometimes traded with the Indians of the region. This exposed the Native Americans to European diseases, to which they had no immunity. Devastating epidemics swept through New England in the first decades of the 1600s. (The Wampanoag had been nearly obliterated. When the Pilgrims landed, they

founded their settlement of Plymouth on the empty site of Patuxet, a formerly thriving Wampanoag village that had suffered 100 percent mortality.)

21. 1. d 2. b, c 3. c 4. d 5. a 6. b

22. 1. skunk 2. moccasin 3. squash 4. toboggan 5. moose

23. Native Americans occupied land communally and often moved from place to place. Also, a farm plot unused by its most recent tenders could be taken over by another vegetable grower. Both of these customs were a complete contradiction of European land ownership/use customs and laws. Indians had no concept of individual land ownership, whereas that concept was central to Europeans. Rather than owning land, Native Americans claimed the right to use the land within the area where they were living. When they signed land treaties with Europeans, Native Americans were usually intending to agree to the Europeans' right to use that land. Paragraphs will vary. Misunderstandings and clashes were inevitable.

24. 1. J, P 2. P 3. P 4. J 5. J 6. P 7. J

25. Paragraphs will vary. Sample answer:
The personality of each colonist would color his or her views. A pessimistic person given to dwelling on the hardships, dangers, and difficulties of life in the colonies, and missing the many centuries of settlement and cultivation in England, might see "a hideous and desolate wilderness." An optimistic and adventurous person would be open to the newness and opportunities of the new land.

26. New England: Massachusetts, New Hampshire, Connecticut, Rhode Island. Middle Colonies: New York, New Jersey, Pennsylvania, Delaware. Southern Colonies: Virginia, Maryland, North Carolina, South Carolina, Georgia. Sentences will vary. New England had thin, rocky soil suitable only for subsistence agriculture, but was rich in

timber and fish. The middle colonies had rich, tillable soil for farming, iron resources, a diverse population, and a mixed economy. The southern colonies was the warmest colonial region. Its economy was largely based on plantation-grown cash crops, such as tobacco and rice; its western back country was an area of subsistence farming.

27. 1. Algonquian for "at the big hill" 2. from the "Virgin Queen," the unmarried Queen Elizabeth 3. for Lord de la Warr, an early governor of Virginia 4. in honor of King Charles I of England 5. Mohican for "at the long tidal river" 6. James, Duke of York, named it after himself 7. for Sir George Carteret, one of the original proprietors, who was from the island of Jersey 8. in honor of Queen Henrietta Maria, wife of King Charles I, who signed the 1632 charter creating the colony 9. for William Penn, the colony's founder

28. Events should be numbered in this order: 7, 2, 3, 5, 1, 8, 4, 6

29. Paragraphs will vary. Sample answer: The advertisement would appeal to a lower-class workingman with little to no hope of securing a job that paid enough to do barely more than support himself, never a family. It would appeal to lower-class women who had little prospect of marriage because men of their low socioeconomic class couldn't afford to marry. The ad is written to entice both of these types of people to make a (supposedly) far better life for themselves in Pennsylvania.

30. 1. e 2. c 3. a 4. d 5. f 6. b

31. 1. Mennonites (also some Quakers) 2. Pilgrims 3. Catholics 4. Quakers 5. Huguenots 6. Jews

32. 1. c 2. f 3. d 4. a 5. e 6. b
Silence Dogood was one of Benjamin Franklin's pseudonyms.

33. 1. indentured servant 2. slave 3. transported convict 4. free immigrant 5. indentured servant 6. slave

34. Answers will vary. Sample answer:
    Your quality of life depends entirely on the type of master you have. If your master is kind and fair, your life is hardworking but equitable by the standards of the time. If your master is indifferent to the conditions of your daily life, mean-spirited, or abusive, your life is one of drudgery, deprivation, and abuse. You have no recourse other than to run away, as long as the master provides (barely) enough food, clothing, and housing to keep you alive.

35. Sentences will vary. Sample answers:
    1. Tobacco was Virginia's first successful cash crop. Profits from tobacco exports transformed struggling Virginia into a successful, thriving colony. 2. Tobacco agriculture was backbreaking, labor-intensive work. Virginia didn't have a large enough labor pool to support multiple large tobacco plantations (tobacco wore out the soil quickly, so large farms were necessary). Tobacco

planters turned to imported slave labor.

36. The following statements should be checked: 1, 3, 4, 7

37. 1. banana 2. gumbo 3. banjo 4. chimpanzee 5. yam 6. voodoo

38. 1. a New England colony 2. a Middle colony, most likely Pennsylvania 3. Virginia, Maryland, or North Carolina 4. Pennsylvania 5. a New England colony, especially Massachusetts 6. South Carolina 7. a New England colony—Rhode Island in particular

39. 1. a 2. b 3. b 4. a 5. b

40. 1. North America 2. Africa 3. North America, Caribbean 4. Europe 5. Europe 6. North America 7. Europe 8. Caribbean 9. North America, Europe 10. Caribbean, Europe 11. North America, Europe 12. Europe 13. Europe, Caribbean 14. Africa, Europe

41. 1. An overwhelming majority of people in Massachusetts were of English origin. In contrast,

the population of Pennsylvania had quite diverse national origins. 2. Massachusetts had been founded by Pilgrims and Puritans from England who for a number of years did not welcome people of other religions or nationalities. Pennsylvania was founded as a haven for free practice of religion and so attracted immigrants from a variety of nations; the high percentage of Germans was due to persecution of a number of religious sects in that nation.

42. These statements should be checked: 2, 4, 5 Sentences will vary. Sample answers:
1. Tobacco cannot be sent outside the British Empire. 2. This is allowed as trade within the Empire, as long as a British (including colonial) ship is used. 3. Foreign ships cannot conduct any of the English colonies' trade. 4. European products imported to the colonies must be sent from England, and on British ships, so this is allowed. 5. Goods that are imported into England must be carried by British ships, and ships of the English colonies are British. (*Note:* none of the wine is unloaded for sale in England.) 6. Two violations: This is a non-British ship importing goods into England, and a non-British ship bringing goods to the colonies.

43. 1. New Englanders had captured Port Royal in Nova Scotia, a center for the Canadian fishing fleet that competed with New Englanders; the treaty ending the war returned Port Royal to the French. 2. Britain obtained Nova Scotia, Newfoundland, and the Hudson Bay area, which was good for the colonists. 3. New Englanders captured Louisburg on Cape Breton Island, by the entrance to the Gulf of St. Lawrence; the treaty ending the war gave Louisburg back to the French. 4. France gave up all claims to North America except two small Canadian islands; this should have been a benefit to the colonists, but the costs of the war prompted Britain to pass measures to

make the colonies pay for part of these costs, which led to the American Revolution.

44. 1. c 2. a 3. d 4. e 5. b
45. Events should be numbered in the following order: 3, 7, 2, 6, 4, 1, 8, 5
46. Paragraphs will vary. Sample paragraph: Colonists at this time thought of themselves as New Yorkers, Virginians, South Carolinians— citizens of their own colonies. They also thought of themselves as British citizens. So Rutledge considered being in England as being in his home country, whereas New York was "foreign." Ironically for Britain, its colonial actions drove colonists to write and meet with one another and in the process begin to develop a national identity. This inspired Patrick Henry to declare at the First Continental Congress in 1774, "I am not a Virginian, but an American."
47. 1. a. All men are created equal. b. All men have inalienable God-given rights (including life, liberty and the pursuit of happiness). c. Governments exist to protect these rights. d. If government fails to protect these rights, the people have the right to change or abolish that government and form a new one. 2. Students' answers will vary. Sharing answers would be a good basis for class discussion.
48. 1. British advantage 2. American advantage 3. American disadvantage 4. American disadvantage 5. British disadvantage 6. British advantage 7. American advantage 8. British disadvantage
49. Paragraphs will vary. Sample paragraph: Washington had a lot of military experience. He became familiar with both British and Indian battle tactics, and he learned how to be a commander. He also knew how to conduct himself as a gentleman, which gained him the respect of the Continental Congress. His dignified demeanor and his deep personal commitment to the revolution drew great

loyalty to him from his troops.

50. 1. b 2. a 3. e 4. d 5. c

51. 1. April 1775; the British retreat from Concord became a rout as colonial militiamen using guerilla tactics shot down hundreds of British soldiers. 2. June 1775; although the British took the hill on their third attempt, they suffered huge casualties—more than 1,000—and the Patriots had proved again that they could stand and fight well. 3. May 1775; Henry Knox brought the fort's cannon to Boston (a remarkable feat); installed overnight on Dorchester Heights, they convinced British General Howe to withdraw his forces from Boston. 4. August and September 1776; Howe readily defeated Washington at Long island, but allowed the American army to slip away to Manhattan; then Howe attacked lower Manhattan (New York City), allowing Washington's army to retreat north. 5. December 1776; Washington's surprise attack routed Hessians, experienced professional soldiers; this provided a large and badly needed boost to American morale.

52. 1. c 2. e 3. b 4. a 5. d

53. The following should be checked: 1, 2, 3, 5, 7, 9, 10, 11, 12

54. Paragraphs will vary. Sample paragraph: The poem gives a very one-sided account of the event. The British commanding officer and his soldiers are cast as bloodthirsty, enjoying the carnage they inflict, grinning over the corpses of the men they have shot. The taunting colonists, who threw rocks at the soldiers, are hailed as guiltless. The poem is designed to manipulate and inflame the emotions of its readers in favor of the revolutionary cause.

55. 1. d 2. c 3. b 4. a 5. e

56. 1. T 2. F (closed it to white settlers, legally, but ineffectively) 3. T 4. F (to the British) 5. T 6. F (was aimed at the Iroquois)

57. 1. S, N 2. N 3. S 4. N 5. S 6. N 7. S 8. S 9. N

10. N

58. 1. preamble 2. amendment 3. compromise 4. ratify

59. 1. Representation based on the state population. (States with large populations supported this.) 2. Equal representation for each state. (States with small populations supported this.) 3. House of Representatives' numbers based on state population, Senate has two senators for every state. (States with medium-sized populations, and states that were seeking a way to solve the dilemma, supported this.) Plan chosen: Connecticut Plan.

60. 1. E 2. L 3. L 4. E 5. J 6. E 7. L 8. L 9. L 10. E

61. 1. Article I, Section 9: Congress cannot outlaw the slave trade before the year 1808. 2. Article I, Section 2: Three fifths of slaves will be counted for these purposes. Students' opinions about these compromises will vary. They would be a good basis for a class discussion.

62. 1. impeachment 2. majority 3. representative 4. veto 5. electoral college

63. Amendment 1: freedoms of religion, speech, press, meeting/demonstrating/objecting to the government. Amendment 2: freedom to keep and bear arms. Amendment 4: freedom from unreasonable searches, and no searches without warrants. Amendment 6: the right to a speedy, public trial by an impartial jury.

64. 1. F—John Jay; 2. AF—Patrick Henry; 3. F—Alexander Hamilton; 4. AF—Thomas Jefferson

65. 1. f 2. a 3. c 4. d 5. e

66. 1. S, W 2. S, W 3. S, W 4. S 5. S, W 6. S, W. 7. W 8. S

67. 1. c 2. a 3. d. The Supreme Court never made ruling b.

68. 1. freedom of speech and of press; First Amendment. 2. Students' opinions will vary. U.S. Representative Matthew Lyon, a Republican from Vermont, was sentenced to four months in jail for writing in a letter that President John Adams had

an "unbounded thirst for ridiculous pomp, foolish adulation, and selfish avarice." He was reelected to Congress while serving his jail term. 3. Opinions and paragraphs will vary.

69. 1. f; Van Buren was born in Kinderhook, New York. 2. d; Jackson's soldiers in the War of 1812 gave him this nickname in recognition of his great toughness (hickory wood is extremely tough). 3. g; Polk was a protégé of Jackson and patterned himself after Old Hickory. 4. a; General Harrison earned this nickname after his army's victory in the Battle of Tippecanoe against the Shawnee. 5. h; As a general in the Mexican War, Scott was always dressed impeccably. 6. b; Taylor's soldiers in the Mexican War gave him this nickname in honor of his informal clothing and manners and his love of getting into the thick of every battle. 7. e; Throughout his political career, Clay excelled at the art of compromise; he was also called the Great Compromiser. 8. c; Tyler became president by accident, after President William Henry Harrison died in office.

70. 1. This Democratic slogan was a nationalistic appeal for taking all of the Oregon Territory, including regions claimed by Great Britain. This slogan especially appealed to western Democrats. 2. This slogan referred to the Battle of Tippecanoe, a great defeat for the Shawnee, which made William Henry "Old Tippecanoe" Harrison, the Whig candidate for president, a national hero. 3. This slogan appealed to opponents of slavery: "free soil" (not slave territory), "free men" (not slaves), "free speech" (freedom of abolitionists to speak out), and "free labor" (not slavery); each phrase dovetails nicely with "Frémont." Explanations will vary.

71. Paragraphs will vary. Sample paragraph: Jonny is President John Quincy Adams, running for reelection. Andrew is Andrew Jackson, running against Adams. John Bull is the symbol of

Daily Warm-Ups: U.S. History

England. "Crimson" suggests the trappings of monarchy. "Down" refers to coverings made of soft, fluffy feathers. "Pelf" means money, riches. All together these words paint a picture of Adams's supposedly sumptuous lifestyle and aristocratic manners. This contrasts with the "brave" General Jackson, defeating Britain at the Battle of New Orleans, forcing Britain to lower its flag ("colors") and paying his troops out of his own pocket (which may or may not be true). The title refers to Andrew Jackson's tough nickname, Old Hickory.

72. Paragraphs will vary. Sample paragraph:
Forces that might have destined expansion include the ever-increasing pressure of an ever-growing population looking for more and more land, a rapidly expanding economy, nationalism and a national security desire to control the continent from east to west without hostile European powers on the western border, and a sense of power and confidence among the American people. European politics and wars that led to the sale of the Louisiana territory to the United States might have played out differently and left Spain and France in possession of Louisiana, with most of the U.S. western border ending at the Mississippi River.

73. Answers will vary. Sample answers:
1. Sentences will vary. Long is describing the Great Plains. For many years, Americans referred to the Plains as "The Great American Desert."
2. This is very inaccurate. The Great Plains became highly productive farmland in the post–Civil War era after needed technological innovations emerged, such as steel-tipped plows, windmills and pumps, and large-scale power equipment, such as thresher/binders, reapers, and combines.

74. 133 days, 4 1/2 months. Delay-causing hazards included natural obstacles (rivers, waterless

stretches, mountains); disease (contagious illnesses that spread through a wagon train); weather (extreme heat and cold, snowstorms, violent thunder/lightning storms); wagon breakdowns and repairs; accidents of all kinds; childbirth and death and burial; need for a day of rest; sometimes, hostile encounters with Native Americans. Delays would add a month or more to the calculation of 4 1/2 months.

75. 1. Sojourner Truth 2. Elizabeth Cady Stanton 3. Harriet Beecher Stowe 4. Mary Lyon

76. 1. F 2. T 3. F 4. T 5. T 6. F 7. T 8. F 9. F 10. T

77. 1. Manifest destiny 2. impressment 3. embargo 4. tariff 5. assimilation

78. 1. c 2. a 3. d 4. b

79. Sentences will vary. Sample answers:
1. Prosser crafted a well-organized plot to seize Richmond, Virginia, in 1800, involving up to several thousand slaves. Two recruits disclosed the plot the day it was to be carried out; Prosser and many of his followers were executed. 2. Vesey, who had bought his freedom, planned a revolt in South Carolina that was exposed in 1822 before it could be carried out. 3. Turner led about 60 fellow slaves in attacks that killed 57 whites, including entire families, in Virginia in 1831. Turner was captured and executed, along with 17 of his followers.

80. "I looked over Jordan"—looking across the Ohio River or Mississippi River. "And what did I see?"—free territory where slavery was not allowed. "Comin' for to carry me home."—to freedom from slavery. "A band of angels"—members of the Underground Railroad. "Comin' after me,"—coming to help me get to free territory. "Comin' for to carry me home."—coming to guide me to freedom in the North or West.

81. Reasons will vary. Sample answers:
Reasons to go would include a burning desire for freedom; personal pride; abusive and cruel treatment; despair at the sale of yourself or a

spouse, children, and/or parents; the arrival of an Underground Railroad conductor such as Harriet Tubman in your vicinity. Reasons to stay might include loyalty to "master" and/or "mistress," the inability or unwillingness of a loved family member to go with you, and/or the likelihood of capture and ensuing dreadful punishment.

82. Developments should be numbered in this order: 3, 5, 1, 4, 7, 2, 6

83. Developments should be numbered in this order: 4, 7, 6, 1, 3, 5, 2

84. 1. In 1811, William Henry Harrison and his army defeated the Shawnee and killed Tenskwatawa (the Prophet). The union of Native Americans that Tecumseh—the Prophet's brother—forged fell apart. 2. In 1814, General Andrew Jackson, his troops, and White Stick Creeks defeated the Red Stick Creeks. The power of the Creeks was crushed. 3. In 1817–1818, General Jackson, his troops, and White Stick Creeks defeated the Seminoles in Florida, including the teenage Osceola. The Seminoles were forced to move to inferior land farther south in Florida. 4. Seminoles fought the U.S. army with guerrilla tactics from 1835–1842. General Jesup's troops treacherously captured Osceola under a flag of truce. Most Seminoles then gave up and moved west to the Indian Territory.

85. Students' paragraph responses will vary. This was the constant dilemma of Native Americans from the time the first Europeans began developing settlements in the 1600s: to fight or yield to superior numbers and firepower. By Tecumseh's time, Native Americans had the fact of innumerable Native American treaties to cede land in return for "always secured" reserved Indian land broken over and over, constantly pushing back Native Americans. A student in this activity might decide this progression was irreversible and the outcome of resistance inevitably defeat, or that

resistance could succeed with an unprecedented union of eastern Indians across the region.

86. Students' paragraphs will vary. Some constitutional experts question whether the executive branch has constitutional authority to enforce a Supreme Court decision, especially one that applies to a state. Under the Constitution, the executive is authorized to enforce laws, not judicial decisions. Also, under the Constitution, the legislative branch is authorized to pass legislation, not enforce judicial decisions about that legislation. This is an interesting illustration of the potential limits of checks and balances and also of the voluntary acceptance of the Supreme Court's ruling under John Marshall on judicial review.

87. Advantages would include regular income, increased purchasing power, jobs available for unskilled laborers and immigrants, and many job openings. Disadvantages would include long hours,

low pay, dangerous working conditions, child labor, and family dislocation or disruption.

88. 1. 4 million; 2. 5 million. 3. Paragraphs will vary. Expanding industry created expanding numbers of jobs. Lots of land was still available, and improved transportation networks—including railroads—allowed immigrants to head directly west to that land. Political and religious freedom drew some, especially after the failed revolutions in Europe. Irish people came in droves after the potato blight hit. Chinese men came for jobs building the western end of the transcontinental railroad.

89. 1. 1820; Calmed things for several decades—Missouri entered as a slave state while Maine entered as free. Drew a line at 36°30' latitude through the territories, with slavery permitted south of the line and banned north of the line. 2. 1850; Calmed things for a while—California entered the Union as a free state; residents of Utah and New Mexico would decide on slavery in

right of the people to alter or abolish governments," and "become(s) destructive of the(se) ends." Abraham Lincoln's statement is in contrast to these principles.

94. 1. popular sovereignty 2. free soil 3. fugitive 4. abolition 5. nullification

95. 1. 1836, slave 2. 1850, free 3. 1845, slave 4. 1846, free 5. 1837, free 6. 1858, free 7. 1859, free 8. 1845, slave 9. 1848, free. More free (six) than slave (three) states entered the Union during these years. After 1845, all the new states were free.

96. 1. South, disadvantage 2. South, advantage 3. North, disadvantage 4. North, advantage 5. South, advantage 6. North, disadvantage 7. North, advantage 8. South, disadvantage

97. Confederates were fighting to protect and preserve their way of life and their freedom to maintain slavery and not be interfered with by the North. They were also fighting for and mostly on their own land, so like the colonists, they were highly motivated. They hoped to hang on and wear down the North.

98. 1. The Southern states are in a state of unlawful rebellion and must be forced back into the Union. The South has brought on the war. 2. The North is trying to force its ways on the South and has refused to allow the South to run its own affairs unmolested. The North has brought on the war.

99. 1. 1861, South 2. 1862, North 3. 1863, North 4. 1862, South 5. 1865, North 6. 1863, North 7. 1863, South. *Bonus answers:* 1. The North is shocked and realizes the secession won't be easy to put down, while the South gets a huge morale boost. 2. The North stops the South's attempt to invade Northern territory, but fails to follow up; the Northern "victory" gives Lincoln an opportunity to issue the Emancipation Proclamation. 3. This is the turning point of the war, in favor of the North. 4. Huge casualties for

both victor and vanquished—20,000 total—shake each side deeply. 5. Lee realizes it is futile to continue fighting. 6. The Union gains control of the Mississippi River. 7. Union morale suffers another big blow, but the South loses one of its best generals, Stonewall Jackson.

100. 1. d 2. a 3. e 4. b 5. c

101. 1. Slaves not freed were slaves in border states, slaves in Union states and territories, and slaves in Confederate territory controlled by the Union. 2. He wanted to keep the border states in the Union, and entice states "in rebellion" to return to the Union.

102. Every statement except 3 should be checked.

103. 1. Tennessee River 2. Cumberland River 3. Mississippi River 4. Louisiana
Sentences will vary. These victories broke the South's control and defense of the Mississippi River and several of its major tributaries. Fort Henry and Fort Donelson commanded their rivers; their capture opened the way for a Union invasion into the Confederate heartland. Vicksburg and Port Hudson commanded the Mississippi in the South. The Confederacy was now split east-west along the Mississippi; the Confederate states west of the Mississippi could no longer send soldiers and war supplies to the Confederate states east of the Mississippi.

104. 1. d 2. e 3. f 4. c 5. a 6. g 7. b

105. Events should be numbered in this order: 5, 2, 7, 4, 1, 6, 3. *Note:* Activity 164 explores the parallels with the 1960s protest movement when women became indignant about men's relegation of them to second-class status and women launched a new women's rights movement.

106. 1. This followed moderate policies favored by Abraham Lincoln; it allowed Southern states to form new governments and elect members of Congress on lenient terms. 2. This put Southern states under military rule, which enforced voting

and other rights for blacks. Scalawags and carpetbaggers captured the most influence.

107. 1. c 2. d 3. b 4. a

108. Events should be numbered in this order: 5, 7, 1, 4, 8, 3, 6, 2

109. 1. e 2. c 3. a 4. d 5. f 6. b

110. 1. F 2. T 3. T 4. F 5. T 6. F

111. Numbers 1, 4, and 5 should be checked.

112. In the second count of the electoral vote, overseen by Congress, Democrats supported Republican Hayes in return for Republican agreement to remove the remaining federal troops from the South and let the Southern states run their own affairs—in other words, to end Reconstruction.

113. 1. b 2. d 3. a 4. c 5. e

114. Students' paragraphs will vary. Reasonable arguments can be made on both sides.

115. 1. c 2. e 3. a 4. f 5. b 6. d

116. Paragraphs will vary. The same question could be asked of Andrew Carnegie, who gave away virtually his entire fortune.

117. 1. It could cut through the tough prairie sod, so that much more land could be farmed. 2. It slashed the cost of fencing that protects crops and livestock. 3. Farmers were now able to draw up water from beneath the Great Plains, where rainfall would not support reliable crops. 4. The combine cuts, threshes, and cleans crops all at once, greatly reducing labor costs.

118. 1. Black Kettle settled peacefully with his Cheyenne people near two different U.S. army forts. U.S. army troops attacked and massacred this group twice, at Sand Creek and at Washita, where Black Kettle was killed. 2. Chief Joseph led his Nez Perce people on a flight to Canada to avoid being forced to leave their land and move to a faraway reservation. The U.S. army stopped the Nez Perce just a few dozen miles from the Canadian border. 3. Red Cloud led his Oglala Sioux against the U.S. army, including total

victory against troops led by Captain Fetterman. Later, he lived with his people on the Pine Ridge reservation. 4. The Paiute Messiah, he started the Ghost Dance movement, a religious revival that swept the Dakota Sioux in 1890 promising a spring renewal of the Plains Indians' lost way of life.

119. Events should be numbered in this order: 3, 7, 5, 9, 2, 6, 1, 8, 4

120. Urban population grew 700 percent, from about 5 million to about 42 million, between 1860 and 1910. It grew at a rate of 5 million every 10 years through 1890, then grew by 10 million per decade between 1890 and 1910.

121. 1. Gave cities on rivers (as most early cities were) everyday commercial links with adjoining cities and regions. 2. Made tall buildings possible; city land is limited, so now can build up rather than out. 3. Made skyscrapers possible, bringing people up to higher-level floors that were not practical to access by just stairs. 4. Urban transportation is much faster, efficient, and comfortable, and streets are no longer so congested and filled with horse manure.

122. 1. 1880—people from northern and western Europe; 1900—people from southern and eastern Europe. 2. Sentences will vary. The rapidly growing industrial economy in the United States meant jobs were readily available for immigrants. Farmlands in the Plains were also readily available. Many immigrants from eastern and southern Europe were fleeing poverty, religious persecution, and/or political unrest. The great wave of immigrants from northern and western Europe had already arrived, and the strong growth of industry in those regions made many jobs available at home and so lessened the motivation for immigration.

123. 1. The AFL was for skilled workers only; Samuel Gompers, its founder and leader, was also the head

of the Cigarmakers Union. 2. The AFL doesn't represent unskilled workers, and it discourages black membership; the Knights were formed to represent this type of worker. 3. The IWW (Wobblies) actively promoted these goals.

124. 1. c 2. f 3. a 4. e 5. b 6. d

125. 1. Woodhull ran for president in 1872 as the Equal Rights Party candidate. She also published a weekly magazine and—shockingly—divorced her husband. 2. Lockwood ran for president in 1884 and 1888 as the candidate of the National Equal Rights Party. She was also allowed to practice law in the 1870s and became the first woman admitted to practice before the Supreme Court. 3. Lease was a radical activist for the Populist Party; she traveled the country in the 1890s giving charismatic speeches. 4. Better known as Mother Jones, she was an outspoken and fearless labor advocate who was arrested numerous times.

126. Supported by: (B/D—farmers; McK/R—business people, bankers, workers); liberal or conservative: (B/D—L, McK/R—C); tariffs: (B/D—low; McK/R—high); regions: (B/D—south, west; McK/R—Northeast); urban/rural: (B/D—urban; McK/R— urban); silver or gold: (B/D—silver; McK/Rep—gold) Paragraphs will vary.

127. The policy most emphatically was not followed. All southern states passed Jim Crow laws that ordered segregation of the races. Blacks and whites were separated on buses and railroads and in public places, such as restaurants, hospitals, prisons, cemeteries, public bathrooms, schools, shows, even public parks and water fountains. Intermarriage was banned. Voting rights were suppressed through poll taxes, literacy tests, and intimidation.

128. 1. check (1876); 2. check (1880s); 3. check (gradual process of improvements; became a craze in the 1890s); 4. no check (c. 1930s); 5. check (after Civil War); 6. no check (Marconi 1901);

7. check (1879); 8. check (no check is acceptable—primitive projected films in theaters began in 1896, but widely popular silent films in theaters bloomed in the early 1900s featuring popular offerings such as *The Great Train Robbery*.); 9. check (1879); 10. check (1895); 11. no check (1918 in the United States); 12. check or no check (Duryea brothers launched first U.S. car in 1893 and electric cars also became available, but cars didn't become common until the 1900s.)

129. 1. b 2. d 3. a 4. c

130. *Note:* Depending on the time available for this activity, you could assign just some rather than all of the names, or different names to different students. 1. Martí led Cuban rebels in a fight for independence from Spain beginning in 1895. 2. General Weyler, nicknamed "Butcher," herded civilians into "reconcentration camps." 3. His newspaper, the *New York Journal*, published sensationalized stories about Weyler's "atrocities"—Spanish cruelty and Cuban suffering. Its reports on the destruction of the U.S.S. *Maine* blamed Spain. 4. He gained national attention for the exploits of the Rough Riders he led at Kettle Hill and San Juan Hill. 5. Navy admiral Dewey's fleet easily destroyed the Spanish fleet in the Philippines. 6. Rebels in the Philippines fought with the Americans against Spain under this leader. When the United States refused to grant Philippine independence, Aguinaldo led his rebel forces in a bitter guerrilla fight against U.S. troops from 1899 to defeat in 1902.

131. 1. E 2. RE 3. RA 4. FP 5. M 6. MD

132. An awareness was beginning to grow that the amount of wild, unsettled land in the United States was not unlimited. The Census Bureau announcement confirmed this. Far-sighted Americans realized that to preserve wilderness in its natural state, exceptional areas had to be

protected as national parks.

133. 1. Whenever the United States judges that conditions in a Latin American nation threaten U.S. economic or security interests, the United States will intervene in that nation's domestic affairs. 2. The United States will control Latin American nations through financial means rather than through the use of U.S. military forces. (In practice, U.S. troops are used along with dollars.) 3. The objective of U.S. foreign policy in Latin America is to support and promote the development of democratic governments. (However, when U.S. interests were threatened, Woodrow Wilson followed the Big Stick policy of intervention.)

134. 1. c 2. d 3. a 4. b

135. 1. This amendment allowed a federal income tax. 2. Ordered direct rather than indirect election of U.S. senators. 3. Outlawed making or selling of alcoholic beverages. 4. Gave U.S. women the right to vote.

136. 1. c 2. f 3. g 4. b 5. d 6. a 7. e

137. 1. He was found guilty of violating the Sedition Act of 1918 for speaking out against U.S. participation in World War I. (He had received a 10-year sentence, but President Harding commuted his sentence to time served on December 25, 1921, a total of 20 months.) 2. Answers will vary. He did break the law, which had been upheld by the U.S. Supreme Court. The Court found that free speech could be limited in wartime if it created a "clear and present danger" to the nation. Students may argue that the Court's decisions in 1919 are wrong and that the Espionage and Sedition Acts were an unconstitutional limit on rights of free speech and of the press.

138. (Another version of the Garner quotation is "a pitcher of warm piss." The quotation may be apocryphal; if not, the plain-spoken Garner might

well have used the saltier term.) 1. The U.S. Constitution provides only that the vice president becomes president when the sitting president dies or otherwise leaves office, and that the vice president is president of the U.S. Senate and can vote on any question only in cases of a tie. 2. Students' responses will vary. The federal government is far larger today, and governing the nation is far more complicated, so the role of the vice president has increased accordingly. Much depends on the use each president chooses to make of each vice president. Vice presidents are usually chosen to balance the ticket and to enhance election prospects, so the relationship between president and vice president may or may not be good.

139. Events should be numbered in this order: 3, 7, 5, 1, 6, 8, 2, 4.

140. Items to be checked: tank, U-boat, warplane, long-range artillery, poison gas. The machine gun was introduced during the Civil War. The other technologies were first used in World War II.

141. Both wars were terribly destructive. Advances in technology did make World War II weapons more deadly. The United States added the world's most deadly weapon, the atomic bomb. Wilson's prediction about another war within another generation was absolutely correct; World War I ended in 1918, and World War II began in 1939.

142. 1. Tin Lizzie 2. speakeasy 3. flapper 4. bootlegger 5. flaming youth
Paragraphs will vary.

143. The Republican presidential campaign in 1900 used "the full dinner pail" slogan. It underscored the fact that the economy under Republican President McKinley was booming. The workman carried a "full dinner pail" to his job every day for his midday meal. "The full garage" underscored the prosperity of the 1920s under Republican presidents Harding and Coolidge. Everyday

families could now afford to own a car and house it in their own garage.

144. Sentences will vary. On radio: Advertising paid for popular radio programs and fueled the rapid development of this new technology, which became exceptionally popular with the American people. On the economy: The little-noticed problems with the U.S. economy that existed in 1928 resulted in the stock market crash of 1929 and the explosion of economic misery during the ensuing Great Depression.

145. 1. Detroit: 2,000%; Chicago: about 500%.
2. Blacks left the South to escape sharecropping, worsening economic conditions, white oppression, and lynch mobs. They headed North for higher wages, better homes, political rights, and less racial discrimination and violence.

146. 1. poetry 2. novels 3. painting 4. music 5. painting 6. music 7. novels 8. poetry

147. The relevant portion of the First Amendment is "Congress shall make no law respecting an establishment of religion, or prohibiting the free exercise thereof." The local and state supreme courts both found Scopes guilty of breaking the law, although the law certainly appears to be a violation of the First Amendment. The case never reached the U.S. Supreme Court.

148. 1. Margaret Sanger 2. Alice Paul 3. Isadora Duncan 4. Jeannette Rankin

149. 1. He was a man of few words, which earned him the nickname, and he became even more silent when he sank into a deep depression after the death of his 16-year-old son. 2. He was an enthusiastic, high-spirited campaigner. 3. He was a mining engineer who made a fortune and then turned to public service. The nickname reflected the public's view that Hoover could capably direct national prosperity.

150. Nativism is xenophobia. White Protestants reacted fearfully to an influx of Catholic and

Jewish immigrants from southern and eastern Europe, and to a wave of Mexican immigration. Nativists claimed that Americans would become a "hybrid" race of "mongrels." The KKK attracted nativists because of its anti-black, anti-Catholic, anti-Semitic, anti-immigrant policies. Sacco and Vanzetti were convicted mainly because they were Italian immigrant anarchists. The immigration restriction acts were public policy expressions of this revived nativism.

151. Events should be numbered in this order: 4, 2, 6, 3, 1, 5.

152. 1. F 2. T 3. T 4. F 5. T 6. F 7. T 8. T

153. 1. b 2. a 3. c 4. a

154. 1. stock market 2. depression 3. margin 4. panic

155. 1. The economy collapsed after the stock market crash of October 29, 1929, and the Great Depression that followed. In 1940, the economy still hadn't recovered from the Great Depression, especially in the area of employment. 2. Between 1940 and 1942, U.S. forces were mobilized. Manufacturing facilities, and therefore employment, expanded to produce war materiel for the Allies, and ultimately for the U.S. military itself. 3. Full-scale military production during the last two years of World War II finally erased the lingering economic effects of the Great Depression.

156. 1A. E 1B. C 2A. C 2B. E 3A. E 3B. C 4A. C 4B. E

157. Events should be numbered in this order: 3, 4, 6, 1, 7, 2, 5.

158. 1. a rapid, overwhelming military attack such as the ones used by Hitler's army; from the German *Blitz*, "lightning," and *Krieg*, "war" 2. an artificial and inferior substitute for something; from the German *Ersatz*, "substitute"; applied during the war to artificial substitutes for things unavailable due to wartime shortages, such as ersatz coffee made from chicory 3. nonsensical jargon used by

wartime bureaucrats, coined by a state official who compared obscure official language with the gobbling of turkeys 4. acronym for **rad**iolo**ca**tor, or **r**adio **detecting and r**anging device, a new technology introduced during the war to detect airplanes in flight 5. a situation marked by errors and/or confusion, and also an error that causes such a situation; from **s**ituation **n**ormal, **all** **f**ouled **up**

159. 1. c 2. a 3. b 4. b

160. 1. Truman gave millions of dollars to help the French fight the communist Vietminh.
2. Eisenhower sent military supplies and a few military "advisers" to help train the South Vietnamese army, which was fighting the communist Vietcong guerrillas. 3. Kennedy increased the number of U.S. troops in Vietnam to 16,000, and some of them began fighting alongside South Vietnamese forces. 4. Johnson increased U.S. troop numbers to 184,000 by the end of 1965 and then up to 538,000 by mid-1968. He began air strikes against North Vietnam in 1964. 5. Nixon resumed bombing North Vietnam and sent U.S. troops into neighboring Cambodia. Also, he began withdrawing U.S. troops from Vietnam. Finally he reached an agreement with North Vietnam and brought the last U.S. troops home in 1973.

161. 1. Opinions will vary. It seems to authorize at least some of the steps taken. But does it authorize bombing North Vietnam, or sending U.S. forces into Cambodia? 2. Answers will vary. This can open a class discussion on justifications put forth by a variety of presidential administrations to garner support for military action. The Iraq war is an obvious parallel.

162. 1. e 2. c 3. a 4. d 5. f 6. b

163. 1. blacks, and blacks with whites, sitting at a whites-only restaurant counter or table and refusing to leave unless served; first and most famous, three black college students at a

Woolworth's lunch counter in Greensboro, North Carolina 2. refusing to use a service or buy certain products from certain sources; example—the Montgomery bus boycott after the Rosa Parks arrest 3. a bus filled with blacks and whites traveling in the South stopping at segregated bus stations and eating places; numerous ones took place, notably in Montgomery, Alabama, when U.S. Attorney General Robert Kennedy intervened 4. policy of engaging in protest without engaging in violence or reacting violently to violent action by authorities; televised police attacks on nonviolent demonstrators in Birmingham and Selma, Alabama, shocked the nation, and the world. Sentences will vary. Black power: Blacks must take pride in their African-American culture and heritage. Black people must fight for their own communities.

164. 1. The men were relegating the women to second-class status. Women's roles were mostly to be support staff—make coffee, distribute protest flyers, run the offices, help carry out the actions the men decided on. Women became very aware of their secondary status in society as a whole. 2. They became angry that the rights of former black male slaves became protected—including the right to vote—while female rights were left out of the new protections. This gave rise to the strong women's rights movement of the later 1800s and early 1900s, mainly focused on securing the right to vote.

165. In *Plessy*, the Court said that "social" discrimination was acceptable, even in the realm of governmentally sponsored schools. In *Brown*, nearly 60 years later, the Court found that separate public school facilities were incapable of providing black children with an equal education due to the stigma of inferiority. Changing social attitudes about segregation and the impact of a good education propelled the change.

166. 1. f 2. e 3. g 4. d 5. a 6. c 7. b
167. 1.e 2. c 3. a 4. d 5. b
168. 1. c 2. a 3. d 4. b
169. Answers will vary but may point to increased fear during perceived crises and to a reasoned trade-off between civil liberties and security.
170. 1. The Tet offensive showed the American people that the United States was not winning the war—that, in fact, the Vietcong and North Vietnamese forces were getting stronger. 2. President Johnson announced he would not run for reelection; he realized opposition to the Vietnam War would sink him. Richard Nixon was elected president, turning the country from a liberal Democratic era to a much more conservative Republican era. 3. Dr. Martin Luther King, Jr., the leader of the civil rights movement, and Robert F. Kennedy, the leading Democratic contender for the presidential nomination, were both assassinated. 4. Chaos reigned in the streets of Chicago outside the Democratic Party presidential convention; there were increasingly disruptive antiwar demonstrations and students protests as well as urban riots.

171. Hair and clothing—1920s, women's hair is bobbed, and women wear short skirts and little underwear; 1960s, men and women wear long hair and colorful costumes with an "ethnic" look. Dance—1920s, dance is vigorous, e.g., the Charleston; 1960s, dance is to rock and roll with a sexual beat. Attitude—1920s, anti-establishment, women's freedom, scorn for Victorian mores; 1960s, anti-establishment, social and sexual freedom. Drug use—1920s, free use of alcohol and tobacco; 1960s, free use of illicit drugs, such as marijuana and psychedelics.

172. 1. This amendment gave the federal government power to set clean air standards. 2. The EPA was established in 1970 to enforce the National Environmental Policy Act of 1969, which required

environmental impact statements for public projects. 3. The Endangered Species Act protected species of creatures that were found to be critically in danger of becoming extinct in the United States. 4. The Water Quality Improvement Act expanded federal authority to control pollution of water, including a state certification process.

173.   1. People became very self-absorbed, embracing trendy methods of soul-searching for self-knowledge and self-awareness, and women dived into women's liberation. 2. People ardently embraced rampant capitalism, the accumulation of wealth, and ostentatious displays of that wealth. Or, as the character Gordon Gekko declared in the popular movie *Wall Street,* "Greed is good!" Answers about the 1990s nickname will vary; have students share their choices in a class discussion.

174.   1. The House of Representatives votes to accuse (or not), the Senate votes to convict (or not), high federal officials of "high crimes and misdemeanors." 2. The House of Representatives drew up three articles of impeachment against Nixon in July 1975 for lying, obstruction of justice, and using government agencies illegally. Nixon resigned before the House voted on the articles. 3. In 1998, the House impeached Clinton—that is, it formally accused him of lying under oath and said that was an impeachable offense. The Senate found him not guilty. 4. Answers will vary. Factors to consider: The charges against Nixon related to criminal actions, and subverting the Constitution, and were broadly nonpartisan. The charges against Clinton related to lying about extramarital sex, and were highly partisan.

175.   Immigration from Europe has dropped steadily and is only a small percentage by 1990. Immigration from both the Americas and Asia increased greatly. (Figures for 1991–2000 are similar to those from 1981–1990.) Factors: Immigration quotas

were removed in 1965, bringing many more Asian immigrants. Immigrants from the Americas, like those from Asia, came for economic and social opportunities. Students' observations could lead to a class discussion about U.S. society as a "melting pot" versus a "salad bowl."

176. 1. Wallace took the votes of Democrats who opposed strong civil rights enforcement away from Humphrey; since Humphrey was only 1% behind Nixon in the vote, the 13% Wallace vote added to the Humphrey column probably would have given the election to Humphrey. 2. Perot siphoned off votes from both Clinton and Bush; his 19% of the vote, distributed between Clinton and Bush could have tipped the election in either direction. 3. Because the popular vote was so close, and because Nader voters presumably would have voted for Gore if Nader had not been in the race,

Nader's presence in the campaign may have cost Gore the overall/electoral victory. (However, Gore would have won the election if he had carried his home state of Tennessee.)

177. Creations will vary. Students should enjoy sharing them with classmates.

178. Events should be numbered in this order: 4, 6, 1, 3, 7, 2, 5.

179. Paragraphs will vary. The language of the resolution seems limited, yet the need to work diligently to keep the United States as safe as possible from global terrorism is a crucial national security concern.

180. Answers and examples will vary.

Turn downtime into learning time!

For information on other titles in the

Daily *Warm-Ups* series,

visit our web site: walch.com